DANIEL'S
PROPHECIES
MADE EASY

All Scripture quotations in this book are taken from the King James Version of the Bible unless otherwise noted.

Daniel's Prophecies Made Easy

Copyright ©2004 by Midnight Call Ministries
Published by The Olive Press a subsidiary of Midnight Call Inc.
Columbia, South Carolina, 29228

Copy Typist: Lynn Jeffcoat
Copy Editor: Susanna Cancassi
Proofreaders: Angie Peters, Susanna Cancassi
Layout/Design: Michelle Kim
Lithography: Simon Froese
Cover Design: Michelle Kim
Title by: Kathy Roland

Library of Congress Cataloging-in-Publication Data

Froese, Arno
        Daniel's Prophecies Made Easy
        ISBN #0-937422-60-6

        1. Prophecy   2.Bible Teaching   3. Christian Living

Printed in the United States of America

Contents

Introduction

❧

The New Testament book of Revelation is closely related to the Old Testament book of Daniel, although the difference in time is approximately 2,500 years.

Daniel is unique among God's prophets because he is the only one who is called "greatly beloved" by the heavenly messenger.

The book of Daniel contains the clearest description of the Gentile nations in relationship to Israel.

Daniel was educated in Babylon during the Diaspora and had proven himself a capable servant not only to a foreign king, but more important, to the God of Israel. He served the Babylonian system with dedication but he never became a part of it. Thus, Daniel serves as a wonderful model for Christians: We are in the world but not of the world.

Although Daniel's name, which means, "God is my judge," was changed to Belteshazzar, which means

"'Bel' protect his life," he retained his identity so the next king called him by his original name, "Daniel." Finally the heavenly messenger said: "Go thy way, Daniel: for the words are closed up and sealed till the time of the end" (Daniel 12:9).

A careful study of Daniel's life shows his complete dedication to the God of Israel and his willingness to serve any king, but not at the cost of his faith in the living God of Israel. That is why Daniel received four important visions recorded for us impartially. He didn't hate his enemies but served them; he had no plans of changing the political realities of his day but trusted in the living God.

Daniel was confident in God and His prophets and he trusted the written Word. He testified: "In the first year of his reign I Daniel understood by books the number of the years, whereof the word of the LORD came to Jeremiah the prophet, that he would accomplish seventy years in the desolations of Jerusalem" (Daniel 9:2).

In spite of his great love for his people, the city of Jerusalem, and the land of Israel, Daniel offered little information regarding Israel's future but went into extensive details about the Gentile world empires. He summarized world history in Chapter 2 with these words: "And in the days of these kings shall the God of heaven set up a kingdom, which shall never be destroyed: and the kingdom shall not be left to other people, but it shall break in pieces and consume all these kingdoms, and it shall stand for ever" (verse

44). Important to realize is that all nations are insignificant when compared to Israel. Isaiah 40:17 even says that all nations "are as nothing; and they are counted to him less than nothing, and vanity."

Regarding Israel's salvation, a heavenly messenger gave this promise: "And at that time shall Michael stand up, the great prince which standeth for the children of thy people: and there shall be a time of trouble, such as never was since there was a nation even to that same time: and at that time thy people shall be delivered, every one that shall be found written in the book" (Daniel 12:1).

Chapter **1**

DANIEL'S DIVINE DECISION

"In the third year of the reign of Jehoiakim king of Judah came Nebuchadnezzar king of Babylon unto Jerusalem, and besieged it. And the Lord gave Jehoiakim king of Judah into his hand, with part of the vessels of the house of God: which he carried into the land of Shinar to the house of his god; and he brought the vessels into the treasure house of his god" (Daniel 1:1–2).

This period marks the beginning of the times of the Gentiles. As an independent nation, Israel ceased to exist, which is confirmed by Jerusalem's destruction.

The prestigious temple in Jerusalem was completed in 1004 B.C. Its dedication is recorded in 2 Chronicles 7:1–2: "Now when Solomon had made an end of praying, the fire came down from heaven, and consumed the burnt offering and the sacrifices; and the glory of the LORD filled the house. And the priests could not enter into the house of the LORD, because the glory of the LORD had filled the LORD's house." How did the people react? "And when all the children of Israel saw how the fire came down, and the glory of the LORD upon the house, they bowed themselves with their faces to the ground upon the pavement, and worshipped, and praised the LORD, saying, For he is good; for his mercy endureth for ever" (verse 3). Solomon expressed Israel's uniqueness in his prayer recorded in 1 Kings 8:53: "For thou didst separate them from among all the people of the earth, to be thine inheritance."

Israel was no longer a light to the Gentiles. It could not function as God had ordained; it had broken its covenant with God and earned the consequences of becoming captive in a foreign land, away from Jerusalem and the land of Israel.

The Jews not only were separated from their nation, their land and their city, but they were in danger of becoming integrated into Babylon, a Gentile nation.

The Broken Covenant

Important to understand is that the covenant was broken by Israel, not by God. Genesis 17:7 says: "I will establish my covenant between me and thee and thy seed after thee in their generations for an everlasting covenant, to be a God unto thee, and to thy seed after thee." God's will is unconditional and His covenant is everlasting.

The next verse clearly expresses God's will: "And I will give unto thee, and to thy seed after thee, the land wherein thou art a stranger, all the land of Canaan, for an everlasting possession; and I will be their God" (Genesis 17:8). He will establish an everlasting covenant that includes the land clearly defined as an eternal possession and the God of creation will be the God of Israel.

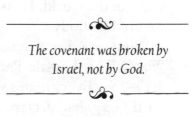

The covenant was broken by Israel, not by God.

The fulfillment of God's covenant with Israel was interrupted but not destroyed. This interruption was a consequence of Israel's continual disobedience and blatant rebellion.

The Bible relates Israel's repeated rebellion against God. The fact that it took until Nebuchadnezzar led the people into captivity testifies of God's patience with His people.

The Church

What a lesson this is for believers of the New Covenant. We are saved by grace and kept by grace, and will enter the heavenly realm by grace. But the way we behave after God has saved us is very important.

The Israelites would not have experienced the trouble, tribulation, hardship and heartbreak if they had listened to God. We too can avoid wasting our time and energy by following in the footsteps of our Savior, who has invited us to follow Him. He is the Light of the world. He is the Head of the Church and we are His Body.

What are the consequences of disobeying His Word? The Apostle Paul answers in 1 Corinthians 3:13–15: "Every man's work shall be made manifest: for the day shall declare it, because it shall be revealed by fire; and the fire shall try every man's work of what sort it is. If any man's work abide which he hath built thereupon, he shall receive a reward. If any man's work shall be burned, he shall suffer loss: but he himself shall be saved; yet so as by fire."

The way believers live on earth will result in one of two possibilities after physical death: reward or loss. Keep in mind that the words "suffer" and "loss" do not relate to salvation but to rewards. The Bible does not reveal the depth of the loss that will be suffered.

The Reward

In the previous chapter, the Apostle Paul quoted the prophet Isaiah: "But as it is written, Eye hath not seen, nor ear heard, neither have entered into the heart of man, the things which God hath prepared for them that love him" (1 Corinthians 2:9).

How do we know we really love God? We know we love Him if our number-one priority is set on heavenly matters. When that's the case, then everything else on earth becomes relatively insignificant.

Asaph, the psalm writer, wrote: "Whom have I in heaven but thee? and there is none upon earth that I desire beside thee" (Psalm 73:25). The desire of this man's heart was clearly directed toward the God of heaven. He concluded Psalm 73 with these words: "But it is

Therefore, the result of a believer's life will be one or the other: a reward or a loss.

good for me to draw near to God: I have put my trust in the Lord GOD, that I may declare all thy works" (verse 28).

This reveals that our testimony is only as good as our drawing near to God and trusting Him.

Israel was segregated from the other nations of the world but never was fully integrated into the Gentile world.

Mixing the Holy with the Unholy

Nebuchadnezzar took "part of the vessels of the house of God." The utensils that had been dedicated to the God of Israel were now in the hands of Babylon. These very utensils became the object of judgment to the next king of Babylon, King Belshazzar, who used them to praise his gods. As a

19

result, we read: "In that night was Belshazzar the king of the Chaldeans slain" (Daniel 5:30). Babylon was judged because it violated God's holy law by using His instruments to worship its own gods. When writing about Babylon's judgment, Jeremiah wrote: "for his device is against Babylon, to destroy it; because it is the vengeance of the LORD, the vengeance of his temple" (Jeremiah 51:11).

Israel's Identity

"And the king spake unto Ashpenaz the master of his eunuchs, that he should bring certain of the children of Israel, and of the king's seed, and of the princes" (Daniel 1:3).

We must not overlook that the Jews who were led captive to Babylon are referred to as the "children of Israel." Subsequently, the Bible teaches that the 12 tribes of Israel were integrated into the tribe of Judah and became Jews.

For example, 2 Chronicles 11:14,16 says: "For the Levites left their suburbs and their possession, and came to Judah and Jerusalem: for Jeroboam and his sons had cast them off from executing the priest's office unto the LORD...And after them out of all the tribes of Israel such as set their hearts to seek the LORD God of Israel came to Jerusalem, to sacrifice unto the LORD God of their fathers."

Chosen To Serve Babylon

King Nebuchadnezzar recognized Israel's value and

integrated the Jews into his inner governmental circle.

Ashpenaz was a key person in this selection process. In *Bibisches Namenlexikon*, Abraham Meister writes that the name Ashpenaz is translated as "oath." Other scholars believe the name means "man of Baal." One thing is certain: Ashpenaz did not believe in the God of Israel, yet he was friendly to the Jews.

Four people are mentioned in this selection process: "Now among these were of the children of Judah, Daniel, Hananiah, Mishael, and Azariah" (Daniel 1:6). These four were to learn the language and the science of Babylon, but in order to do so their names had to be changed.

Verse 7 says: "Unto whom the prince of the eunuchs gave names: for he gave unto Daniel the name of Belteshazzar; and to Hananiah, of Shadrach; and to Mishael, of Meshach; and to Azariah, of Abednego." The powers of darkness were at work. The royal children of Israel would lose their Jewish identity if they became Babylonians. So, how would the Scripture that said the Messiah would come from the house of David be fulfilled?

Their name changes were rather subtle:

Hebrew

Daniel – "God is my judge."

Hananiah – "Yahweh is merciful."

Mishael – "Who is like God?"

Azariah – "Jehovah helped."

Babylonian

Belteshazzar – "Baal protect the king" (Bel – the national

21

god of Babylon).

Shadrach – "Word of Aku" (moon god).

Meshach – "Who is like Aku?" (moon god).

Abednego – "Servant of Nebo" (god of wisdom).

This is a clear picture of the great deceiver, who tries to change the genuine into an imitation. Only these four Jewish men are mentioned, yet they carry great prophetic weight for Israel and the Church.

The danger seen here is an attempt to "Babylonianize" the Jews and destroy their identity. According to verse 3, they were descendants of the kings of Israel, so one would think a name change was a great honor because these men were specially chosen.

The danger seen here is an attempt to "Babylonianize" the Jews and destroy their identity.

No doubt Daniel and his friends were believers in the God of Israel. They knew Scripture, particularly what Jeremiah the prophet had written regarding Jerusalem and Judah. They knew Nebuchadnezzar would conquer Judah and destroy Jerusalem. They easily could have thought it God's will that their nation be destroyed. If indeed it was, it might have been logical for them to say, "Why not become Babylonians?" But this was not the case with Daniel and his friends.

Since they knew Scripture, they understood that God had separated Israel from all other nations.

Exodus 11 says, "that ye may know how that the LORD doth put a difference between the Egyptians and Israel" (verse 7). Daniel was faithful to his God because he knew Him as the God of prophecy; therefore, all the Lord had said through the prophets would come to pass.

The Election Process

Verse 4 lists the requirements for being selected: "Children in whom was no blemish, but well favoured, and skilful in all wisdom, and cunning in knowledge, and understanding science, and such as had ability in

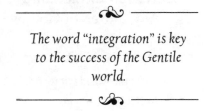

The word "integration" is key to the success of the Gentile world.

them to stand in the king's palace, and whom they might teach the learning and the tongue of the Chaldeans." This verse reveals that Nebuchadnezzar recognized the importance of having representatives from the nations he had conquered as part of the decision-making process of his government. This is typical of the Babylonian spirit even today. The word "integration" is key to the success of the Gentile world.

However, the God of Israel works in the opposite direction. He has no desire for His people to become integrated; He works through segregation. God made His intention known through Moses: "For thou art an holy people unto the LORD thy God, and the LORD hath chosen thee to be a peculiar people unto himself, above all the nations that are upon the earth" (Deuteronomy 14:2). The next verse says: "Thou shalt not eat any abominable thing" (Deuteronomy 14:3). That's where Daniel differed, and he sought to remain that way. He was completely aware that God had selected and separated a people for His name, so he acted in accordance with that conviction.

Christian Citizenship

As children of God, we must never allow ourselves to become integrated spiritually with the nation in which we live. We are in the world but not of the world. We work to earn a living,

We are in the world but we are not of the world.

and we eat, drink, buy and sell, but we must always be fully conscious of the fact that we are only temporary citizens of our country.

Remembering this spiritual truth is an absolute must during these endtimes as we see the nations uniting under the spirit of Babylon, creating an unprecedented powerful, prosperous and peaceful society.

However, those who know the prophetic Word believe this peace, security and prosperity are only temporary. Why? Second Corinthians 4:18 answers: "While we look not at the things which are seen, but at the things which are not seen: for the things which are seen are temporal; but the things which are not seen are eternal."

Dear friend, be careful that nationalistic spirits do not sway you. They never will lead to the peace that passes all understanding. For example, your American citizenship will be totally useless when our Lord returns. Actually, you will be ashamed because of your national pride, fanatic patriotism and conviction that your nation was special, or better than the others. It will be revealed in the presence of the Lord that the devil and his demons were the actual leaders of your country.

Pray the Lord will hasten the building of His Church and that He will use each and every one of us as we spread the wonderful message that only Jesus saves and that real peace — eternal peace — will only be realized when the Prince of Peace rules!

A Rock-Solid Decision

"But Daniel purposed in his heart that he would not defile himself with the portion of the king's meat, nor with the wine which he drank: therefore he requested of the prince of the eunuchs that he might not defile himself" (Daniel 1:8).

This verse reveals that the key to Daniel's being blessed was his refusal to defile himself. Scripture says he "purposed in his heart," meaning he made a conscious decision that came from his heart. And we read that God immediately reacted to Daniel's faithfulness: "Now God had brought Daniel into favour and tender love with the prince of the eunuchs" (verse 9). The Bible doesn't say Daniel became favored of the prince and then decided not to defile himself; his decision to follow and be faithful to the God of Israel was made first. This mighty scriptural truth should deeply penetrate our hearts. We must get our priorities in order. The Lord will guide us continuously when we follow Him wholeheartedly. We don't act in response to our circumstances when we are following the Lord. When we do so, we can exclaim with joy and confidence as David once did: "Yea, though I walk through the valley of the shadow of death, I will fear no evil: for thou art with me; thy rod and thy staff they comfort me" (Psalm 23:4).

"Yea, though I walk through the valley of the shadow of death, I will fear no evil: for thou art with me; thy rod and thy staff they comfort me" (Psalm 23:4).

Greatly Beloved

Daniel loved God above all else. So it is no surprise we read three times that God loved him: "for thou art greatly beloved" (Daniel 9:23); "a man greatly beloved" (Daniel 10:11); "O man greatly beloved" (Daniel 10:19).

Daniel, the Jewish captive in the land of Babylon, is an image of the One who was to come: the greatest Jew of all time, the Lord Jesus Christ. We read the Father's testimonial words on earth: "This is my beloved Son, in whom I am well pleased" (Matthew

3:17). Hebrews 10:7 explains why the Father was pleased: "Then said I, Lo, I come (in the volume of the book it is written of me,) to do thy will, O God." That is the expression of perfect fellowship, total unity and absolute joyful obedience to God's will.

Our Salvation and Future

This eternal and divine love has been extended through the Son to the entire world. Thus, we read: "For God so loved the world, that he gave his only begotten Son, that whosoever believeth in him should not perish, but have everlasting life" (John 3:16). Simple faith in Jesus Christ and His accomplished work on Calvary's cross opens to the sinner the source of immeasurable grace. The Bible says: "For by grace are ye saved through faith; and that not of yourselves: it is the gift of God: Not of works, lest any man should boast" (Ephesians 2:8–9). If you believe Jesus died for your sins and arose on the third day for your justification, then you are guaranteed everlasting life!

But there is more: Jesus not only died, fully atoning for our sins, rising from the dead, and ascending into heaven, but He also promised to come again. Hebrews 9:28 says: "So Christ was once offered to bear the sins of many; and unto them that look for him shall he appear the second time without sin unto salvation."

The holiday we traditionally call Easter is really a victory celebration over sin, death and condemnation. The blood of the Lamb has washed away our sins. Death has been swallowed up in victory, and there is no more condemnation for those who are in Christ.

But there is even more: Now we look to the future with great anticipation and joy for the return of our Redeemer: Jesus, the Son of God.

When the Apostle Paul wrote to the church at Thessalonica, he mentioned one condition required in order to participate in the Rapture: "For if we believe that Jesus died and rose again, even so them also which sleep in Jesus will God bring with him" (1 Thessalonians 4:14). The Church's completion on earth is tied to the completion of Christ's work on earth: namely, His death and resurrection.

Verses 16–18 explain what the completion of the Church will be like: "For the Lord himself shall descend from heaven with a shout, with the voice of the archangel, and with the trump of God: and the dead in Christ shall rise first: Then we which are alive and remain shall be caught up together with them in the clouds, to meet the Lord in the air: and so shall we ever be with the Lord. Wherefore comfort one another with these words."

Daniel determined in his heart not to sin against God. May we, as individuals, make that decision anew, or even for the first time. Jesus said: "If any man serve me, let him follow me; and where I am, there shall also my servant be: if any man serve me, him will my Father honour" (John 12:26).

The Wisdom of God

Wisdom comes from fearing God. It must not be compared to education or intelligence. Wisdom cannot be obtained through study at the world's best universities. The wisdom the Bible speaks of is knowledge granted by God to man. One of the most fundamental truths for us to know is that our days are numbered. We are on earth for only a short time. When our days have expired we will enter eternity, which is timeless. Moses, who recognized God's ways, explained in Psalm 90:12: "So teach us to number our days, that we may apply our hearts unto wisdom." Luther provided a more direct translation: "Teach us to consider that we must die so we may attain wisdom."

David, another great man of the Bible, wrote, "LORD, make me to know mine end, and the measure of my days, what it is; that I may know how frail I am" (Psalm 39:4). He concluded with these words: "verily every man at his best state is altogether vanity" (verse 5).

From today's perspective we might say this man had low self-esteem and recommend that he have a few sessions with a psychologist to rebuild his self-worth. But that is just the opposite of wisdom, which makes the recipient recognize his lost position before the living God.

Furthermore, we read: "The fear of the LORD is the beginning of wisdom: a good understanding have all they that do his commandments: his praise endureth for ever" (Psalm 111:10). Only those who have had an encounter with God recognize their own corruptness and fear the Lord as a result. Such a person has stepped onto the pathway of "the beginning of wisdom."

Solomon, the wisest of all the kings of the world, confirmed this: "The fear of the LORD is the beginning of wisdom: and the knowledge of the holy is understanding" (Proverbs 9:10).

Daniel's Divine Decision

Although there is no record of Daniel opposing his new name, we do read that as a Jew he wanted to continue to practice kosher behavior. In other words, he did not want to eat and drink the same food and drinks as the others. But that caused a problem: "And the prince of the eunuchs said unto Daniel, I fear my lord the king, who hath appointed your meat and your drink: for why should he see your faces worse liking than the children which are of your sort? then shall ye make me endanger my head to the king?" (Daniel 1:10). Obviously, the king's dietary law was designed to improve the appearance of those candidates. But Daniel answered: "Prove thy servants, I beseech thee, ten days; and let them give us pulse to eat, and water to drink. Then let our coun-

Only he who has had an encounter with God recognizes his own corruptness and fears the Lord as a result.

tenances be looked upon before thee, and the countenance of the children that eat of the portion of the king's meat: and as thou seest, deal with thy servants. So he consented to them in this matter, and proved them ten days. And at the end of ten days their countenances appeared fairer and fatter in flesh than all the children which did eat the portion of the king's meat" (verses 12–15).

Prepared for Service

Now we should begin to understand why God used Daniel to pass on such a tremendous wealth of information that reaches

Anyone who wishes to understand eschatology is required to study the book of Daniel.

all the way to our times and even to eternity: he was faithful in every detail. Anyone who wishes to understand eschatology is required to study the book of Daniel.

We have already dealt with verse 8, which states that Daniel decided not to defile himself. He would serve the king and the country to where he was deported, but his priority was to serve the God of Israel! Scripture doesn't say anything about what his three friends had decided, but obviously they agreed with him. Daniel was able to lead his friends because of his complete surrender to God.

Next we read in Daniel 1:17: "As for these four children, God gave them knowledge and skill in all learning and wisdom: and Daniel had understanding in all visions and dreams." These four young men were filled with the wisdom of God. They were skillful in wisdom, cunning in knowledge and had an understanding of science like no other.

The Test

The time for the test came three years later. "And the king communed with them; and among them all was found none like Daniel, Hananiah, Mishael, and Azariah: therefore stood they before the king. And in all matters of wisdom and understanding, that the king inquired of them, he found them ten times better than all the magicians and astrologers that were in all his realm" (Daniel 1:19–20).

That is the secret to living a victorious life on earth, attained by grace through total dedication to the Lord. Jesus put it this way: "But seek ye first the kingdom of God, and his righteousness; and all these things shall be added unto you" (Matthew 6:33). May the Lord grant you this deep desire to please Him as you decide to follow Him in all that you are and in all that you do. Our heavenly Father is seeking those who are able to communicate the reality and the truth of the eternal Word of God through their deeds, their words and their lives.

"But seek ye first the kingdom of God, and his righteousness; and all these things shall be added unto you" (Matthew 6:33).

THE GENTILE IMAGE

"And in the second year of the reign of Nebuchadnezzar Nebuchadnezzar dreamed dreams, wherewith his spirit was troubled, and his sleep brake from him. Then the king commanded to call the magicians, and the astrologers, and the sorcerers, and the Chaldeans, for to shew the king his dreams. So they came and stood before the king. And the king said unto them, I have dreamed a dream, and my spirit was troubled to know the dream" (Daniel 2:1–3).

Chapter 2 reveals why Daniel had to be ten times better: He was to save the scientists of Babylon, himself and his friends and reveal the future of the world of Gentile nations to the king.

Important to mention again is that Daniel's beginning was grounded in his decision to say "yes" to God and "no" to sin: "Daniel purposed in his heart that he would not defile himself." And as a result, the king "found them ten times better" than the rest. Daniel was prepared for the next step.

An Impossible Request

The king made an unreasonable request. Not only did he expect an interpretation of his dream, but he also expected the magicians, astrologers, sorcerers and Chaldeans (his political advisers) to tell him about what he had dreamed.

Even more illogical was Nebuchadnezzar's temper tantrum: "if ye will not make known unto me the dream, there is but one decree for you: for ye have prepared lying and corrupt words to speak before me, till the time be changed: therefore tell me the dream, and I shall know that ye can shew me the interpretation thereof" (Daniel 2:9).

His political advisers tried to reason with him: "It is a rare thing that the king requireth, and there is none other that can shew it before the king, except the gods, whose dwelling is not with flesh" (verse 11). But the next two verses say: "For this cause the king was angry and very furious, and commanded to

34

destroy all the wise men of Babylon. And the decree went forth that the wise men should be slain; and they sought Daniel and his fellows to be slain" (verses 12–13).

The helplessness of these magicians, astrologers, sorcerers and Chaldeans is vividly illustrated in these 13 verses. There was nothing they could do; there was no use in trying to reason with the king. Their future was sealed; there was no way out.

Today's Prophets

Incidentally, this reminds us of our modern world in which educated men try to tell the future. Countless experts who have studied finance and economy attempt to forecast the future. Countless newsletters claim to be able to help us decide what financial investments are best. Do these people really know the future? It's safe to assume that if they really had the facts, they would keep them to themselves and increase their own wealth and power. The truth is, nobody knows the future.

Not even a simple weather forecast is reliable. It's almost comical how the local meteorologists try to forecast the weather just for the next day. They show satellite images of the entire nation, in some cases of the entire world, and explain what weather has already transpired. But we're not interested in all that; we want to know if the sun will shine or if it will rain tomorrow. In order to avoid the embarrassment of making an inaccurate forecast, the meteorologists say there is a "chance" of rain or a "chance" of sunshine. In other words, they're saying, "I don't know, I'm only guessing." Thus, the future is hidden because it has not yet been made visible.

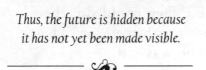

Thus, the future is hidden because it has not yet been made visible.

Declaring the Beginning from the End

How different is the Word of God! God's own testimony was recorded by the prophet Isaiah: "Remember the former things of old: for I am God, and there is none else; I am God, and there is none like me, Declaring the end from the beginning, and from ancient times the things that are not yet done, saying, My counsel shall stand, and I will do all my pleasure" (Isaiah 46:9–10). He adds: "I have even from the beginning declared it to thee; before it came to pass I shewed it thee: lest thou shouldest say, Mine idol hath done them, and my graven image, and my molten image, hath commanded them" (Isaiah 48:5). The future is history to Him, just as history is future to God because He is timeless.

Daniel trusted in the One who could declare things before they became visible.

Daniel knew this God; he knew Isaiah's writings and he trusted in the One who could declare things before they became visible.

The Deciding Moment

The death sentence was also pronounced upon Daniel and his friends. When the executioners were looking for them, Daniel appeared and made this courageous statement: "Why is the decree so hasty from the king? Then Arioch made the thing known to Daniel" (Daniel 2:15).

Time to Pray

"Then Daniel went in, and desired of the king that he would give him time, and that he would shew the king the interpretation" (verse 16). Apparently his request was granted. "Then Daniel went to his house, and made the thing known to Hananiah, Mishael, and Azariah, his companions: That they would desire mercies of the God of heaven concerning this secret; that Daniel and his fellows should not perish with the rest of the wise men of Babylon" (verses 17–18). Why did Daniel call for a prayer meeting? Because he knew this case belonged to the God of heaven, the One of whom King Nebuchadnezzar later testified: "the most High ruleth in the kingdom of men, and giveth it to whomsoever he will, and setteth up over it the basest of men" (Daniel 4:17).

Daniel's faith in the living God was remarkable; he was able to make this request because of his relationship with the God of Israel. Then he went to his knees in prayer and presented his case to the God of heaven.

What was the result? "Then was the secret

revealed unto Daniel in a night vision. Then Daniel blessed the God of heaven" (verse 19).

In his prayer of thanksgiving Daniel revealed something that still applies today: "And he changeth the times and the seasons: he removeth kings, and setteth up kings: he giveth wisdom unto the wise, and knowledge to them that know understanding" (verse 21).

God Rules the Devil's World

Ultimate authority still lies in God's hands. Although the prince of darkness rules the world, the Lord has reserved the final say for Himself. He removes and installs governments. For that reason, the Holy Spirit instructed the Apostle Paul to admonish Christians to be subject to their prevailing government: "Let every soul be subject unto the higher powers. For there is no power but of God: the powers that be are ordained of God" (Romans 13:1).

Although the prince of darkness rules the world, the Lord has reserved the final say for Himself.

Revelation from On High

Little is revealed about Daniel's prayer, but his thanksgiving to God for answering his prayer is detailed: "He revealeth the deep and secret things: he knoweth what is in the darkness, and the light dwelleth with him. I thank thee, and praise thee, O thou God of my fathers, who hast given me wisdom and might, and hast made known unto me now what we desired of thee: for thou hast now made known unto us the king's matter" (verses 22–23).

Now with confidence in the God of Israel Daniel was able to request permission to approach the king. As Daniel stood before Nebuchadnezzar, he heard the king say: "Art thou able to make known unto me the dream which I have seen, and the interpretation thereof?" (verse 26). This was a golden opportunity for Daniel to shine in the king's presence. Instead, Daniel did not speak of himself but defended his colleagues who were destined to die: "The secret which the king hath demanded cannot the wise men, the astrologers, the magicians, the soothsayers, shew unto the king" (verse 27). The king and his host of counselors and advisers were helpless. The king's request was beyond human capability, intelligence and understanding. Daniel continued: "But there is a God in heaven that revealeth secrets, and maketh known to the king Nebuchadnezzar what shall be in the latter days. Thy dream, and the visions of thy head upon thy bed, are these; As for thee, O king, thy thoughts came into thy mind upon thy bed, what should come to pass hereafter: and he that revealeth secrets maketh known to thee what shall come to pass. But as for me, this secret is not revealed to me for any wisdom that I have more than any living, but for their sakes that shall make known the interpretation to the king, and that thou mightest know the thoughts of thy heart" (verses 28–30). Again, Daniel recognized his own limited understanding. There wasn't an ounce of pride in this young Jewish man; he gave God the glory.

There wasn't an ounce of pride in this young Jewish man; he gave God the glory.

The Gentile World

Daniel revealed the dream and the interpretation to King Nebuchadnezzar, thereby showing the history of the entire Gentile world.

We would do well today to follow in Daniel's footsteps and ignore political debates and the boastful speeches of the world's leaders and their power brokers and simply realize the truth of the prophetic Word.

There are only four Gentile superpowers on earth. Their value is represented by gold, silver, brass and iron. But ultimately, they will be "broken to pieces together, and [become] like the chaff of the summer threshingfloors; and the wind carried them away" (Daniel 2:35).

Those words are like an ointment to our souls and cold water to the thirsty; it is peace to the spirit that passes all understanding. God will take care of His creation, no matter how powerful these men think they are, and He will establish His righteousness according to His law.

The prophet Isaiah wrote these inspired words concerning the nations: "All nations before him are as nothing; and they are counted to him less than nothing, and vanity" (Isaiah 40:17). My dear friends, that is the value of this entire world and all its glory, greatness and power. Therefore, now more than ever, we should follow the One who holds the entire world in His hands. We do not need to fear any developments taking place on this earth, nor do we need to place much stock in what world leaders say. Authority lies with the Creator of heaven and earth. Today we should wholeheartedly dedicate ourselves to His service like Daniel, who determined in his heart that he would not defile himself.

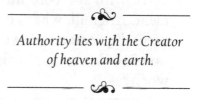

Authority lies with the Creator of heaven and earth.

The Image of the Nations

"Thou, O king, sawest, and behold a great image. This great image, whose brightness was excellent, stood before thee; and the form thereof was terrible. This image's head was of fine gold, his breast and his arms of silver, his belly and his thighs of brass. His legs of iron, his feet part of iron and part of clay. Thou sawest till that a stone was cut out without hands, which smote the image upon his feet that were of iron and clay, and brake them to pieces. Then was the iron, the clay, the brass, the silver, and the gold, broken to pieces together, and became like the chaff of the summer threshingfloors; and the wind carried them away, that no place was found for them: and the stone that smote the image became a great mountain, and filled the whole earth" (Daniel 2:31–35). This dream shows the entire Gentile world and the establishment of God's kingdom on earth.

The four Gentile superpowers are: 1) Babylon; 2) Persia; 3) Greece; and 4) Rome. Analyzing this from today's perspective, we see we are living in the iron-clay empire. However, we would probably disagree with the definition of quality of the government. After all, what's better than democracy? So the natural question follows: Why does the Word of God say Babylon's empire is the best and ours is the worst?

Before we go any further, it may be necessary to explain that when the Bible speaks about the iron-clay government, it means the Romanized world, which existed when Jesus was born and which encompasses the fundamental laws and principles still actively observed by virtually the entire world.

The Roman World

The Roman world is the last empire, and contrary to popular belief, it never ceased to exist. Besides Europe, all the new countries have been built on Roman principles established by Europeans (Romans). It may be helpful to quote a few pages from my book *Saddam's Mystery Babylon*, which featured the following excerpts from the July 19, 1997 issue of *National Geographic*:

Roman Origins

We know that early on, the Romans were ruled by the Etruscans, a powerful nation of central Italy. Chafing under an often-brutal monarchy, the leading families of Rome finally overthrew the Etruscan kings — a revolution that would influence, some 2,200 years later, the thinking of Thomas Jefferson and George Washington.

In the year 244 AUC (that is, 509 B.C.) the patrician families of Rome set up a quasi-representative form of government, with a pair of ruling consuls elected for a one-year term. This marked the beginning of the Roman Republic, a form of government that would continue until Julius Caesar crossed the Rubicon 460 years later. Those five centuries were marked by increasing prosperity and increasing democracy.

—National Geographic, July 1997, P.15

This early democratic system was barely different than ours is today. The article continues:

How About "Fat-Cat Contributors?"

By the second century B.C. the right to vote was so firmly established among the plebelans that Rome developed a vigorous political system – one that would not be unfamiliar to citizens of a modern democracy. There were parties and factions, fat-cat contributors, banners and billboards, negative advertising, and a pundit class to castigate the pols.

—National Geographic, July 1997, p.21

The Romans granted rights but requested duties just like modern democracy.

Rights and Duties of Citizens

Within the broad sweep of uniformity, Roman administration at the local level was flexible, tolerant, and open. When Rome conquered a new province, the defeated general and his army were carted away in chains; almost everyone else came out ahead. The local elite was given positions in the Roman hierarchy. Local businesses gained the benefit of Roman roads, water systems, the laws of commerce and the courts. Roman soldiers guarded the town against pirates and marauders. And within a fairly short period, many of the provincial residents would be made *cives Romani* — citizens of Rome — with all the commensurate rights and duties.

—National Geographic, July 1997, p.30

No one less than Augustus actively supported the Roman pro-life movement.

Anti-Abortion

Augustus used all the tools of governing. Concerned about a decline in the birthrate, he employed both the stick (a crackdown on abortion) and the carrot (tax incentives for big families). To see if his policies were effective he took a census of his empire now and then.

'Thus it did in fact come to pass in those days that there went out a decree from Caesar

Augustus that all the world should be registered.'
And just as St. Luke's Gospel tells us, this hap-
pened 'when Quirinius was governor of Syria,' in
A.D. 6.

Under Roman rule, "world citizenship" was real
and prosperity greatest.

Citizen of the World

History recalls Marcus Aurelius (161–180), the
philosopher-king who maintained perspective in
the midst of imperial splendor: 'As the Emperor,
Rome is my homeland; but as a man, I am a citizen
of the world...Asia and Europe are mere dots on
the map, the ocean is a drop of water, mighty
Mount Athos is a grain of sand in the universe.'
Even the cynical Gibbon had to flip his hat: 'If a
man were called to fix the period in the history of
the world, during which the condition of the
human race was most happy and prosperous, he
would, without hesitation, name that which
elapsed from [A.D. 96 to 180]' — That is, the era of
those 'Five Good Emperors.'

–*National Geographic*, July 1997, P.35

Today's democracies could not function without
Roman law.

Literacy and Law

The English historian Peter Salway notes that
England under Roman rule had a higher rate of lit-
eracy than any British government was able to

achieve for the next 14 centuries. One of the most important documentary legacies the Romans left behind was the law — the comprehensive body of case law that some scholars consider our greatest inheritance from ancient Rome.

The ideal of written law as a shield — to protect individuals against one another and against the awesome power of the state — was a concept the Romans took from the Greeks. But it was Rome that put this abstract notion into daily practice, and the practice is today honored around the world.

–*National Geographic*, August 1997, p.62–63

Ancient Rome was concerned with a citizen's liberty.

Innocent Until Proven Guilty

The emperor Justinian's monumental compilation of *The Digests, the Institutes, and the Revised Code*, completed in A.D. 534, has served as the foundation of Western law ever since. Two millennia before the Miranda warnings, the Romans also established safeguards to assure the rights of accused criminals. We can see this process at work in the case against the Christian pioneer St. Paul, as set forth in the New Testament in the Acts of the Apostles.

In chapter 22 of Acts, Paul is brought before a Roman magistrate on criminal charges — apparently for something like 'provoking a riot.' The police are just about to beat and jail him when

46

Paul pipes up that he is a Roman citizen. That changes everything, and he is permitted to remain free pending a trial.

Festus responds, in chapter 25, with a lecture on legal rights: 'Is it not the Roman custom to hand over any man before he has faced his accusers and has had an opportunity to defend himself against their charges?'

–National Geographic, August 1997, p.68

America's democratic system is clearly modeled after the Roman Republic.

Rome – U.S.A.

The Roman process of making laws also had a deep influence on the American system. During the era of the Roman Republic (509 to 49 B.C.) lawmaking was a bicameral activity. Legislation was first passed by the *comitia*, the assembly of the citizens, then approved by the representative of the upper class, the senate, and issued in the name of the senate and the people of Rome. Centuries later, when the American Founding Fathers launched their bold experiment in democratic government, they took republican Rome as their model. Our laws, too, must go through two legislative bodies. The House of Representatives is our assembly of citizens, and, like its counterpart in ancient Rome, the U.S. Senate was originally designed as a chamber for the elite (it was not until the 17th Amendment, in 1913, that ordinary people were allowed to vote for their senators).

Impressed by the checks and balances of the Roman system, the authors of American government also made sure that an official who violated the law could be "impeached," a word we take from the Roman practice of putting wayward magistrates *in pedica*.

The reliance on Roman structures at the birth of the United States was reflected in early American popular culture, which delighted in drawing parallels between U.S. leaders and the noble Romans.

A larger-than-life statue of Washington in a toga and sandals is still on exhibit at the National Museum of American History in Washington, D.C.

–National Geographic, August 1997, p.70

These historical quotations show that Rome has never really ceased to dominate the world.

Rome will continue to lead the world until the masses have become captivated by peace, success, and prosperity under the guise of democracy led by the Antichrist.

A Model for the World?

I ran across an article in the *Financial Times* entitled: "Europe is the new role model for the world." Here are some excerpts:

It is tempting to dismiss Jeremy Rifkin as yet another practitioner of 'futurology'. As president of the Washington-based Foundation on Economic

Trends, he has recently proclaimed the promise of hydrogen power, the disappearance of work, the sanctity of animal rights and the advent of a global network society. Now comes the European Dream.

But sometimes even futurologists get it right. Just when Europe is being dismissed as a power in terminal decline, Rifkin advances a compelling case for its ascendancy. 'While the American Spirit is tiring and languishing in the past,' Rifkin proclaims, 'A new European Dream is being born.' Against America, Europe 'emphasizes community relationships over individual autonomy, cultural diversity over assimilation, quality of life over the accumulation of wealth, sustainable development over unlimited material growth, deep play over unrelenting toil, and universal human rights.'

European egalitarianism manifests itself most clearly in the social welfare state. Each European is guaranteed a minimum standard of living, not just in cash, but through daycare, unemployment insurance, pensions and healthcare — all far from universal in America. Greater social redistribution and infrastructure permits poorer Europeans to lead a more balanced life. Rifkin rightly notes that Europeans' broad conception of human rights, encompassing socio-economic, cultural and environmental entitlements, is far more attractive than the narrower American conception of human rights as political liberties.

'Whereas Americans define freedom as autonomy and mobility, which requires amassing wealth,' Rifkin observes, 'Europeans define freedom in community — in belonging, not belongings.' Europeans make time for culture. Americans, who view 'idleness to be almost a sin, like sloth,' now work on average 10 weeks more per year than Germans, five weeks more than Britons — more even than the famously workaholic Japanese. This European concern for cultural diversity is likely to resonate across the developing world.

Europeans remain the strongest proponents of universal human rights and the European Union is a multilateral model for the globe, making Europe more attractive to a generation 'anxious to be globally connected and at the same time locally embedded.'

The European Dream should be required reading on both sides of the Atlantic. To Americans it sounds the alarm. At the height of the supposed unipolar dominance of the US, fewer and fewer foreigners view it as an attractive model for constitutions, companies or communities. To Europeans, Rifkin issues the challenge of global leadership.

Europe is really 'best positioned between the extreme individualism of America and the extreme collectivism of Asia to lead the way into the new age'

Financial Times, 10/6/04, p. 17

Religion and Democracy

To further emphasize that Rome, and its religiously motivated democracy is, in fact, alive, let us consider an excerpt from Samuel J. Andrews' book, *Christianity and Anti-Christianity in their Final Conflict:*

> The multitude is made familiar with its principles through magazines and newspapers, through lectures and the pulpit. Its prevalence is shown in the rapidity with which such systems as those of Christian Science, Mental Science, Theosophy, and others kindred to them, have spread in Christian communities, for all have a Pantheistic basis. The moral atmosphere is full of its spirit, and many are affected by it unawares. What shall we say of its diffusion in the future? To judge of this we must look upon its spread from another point of view, and consider its affinity with Democracy.
>
> It is not to be questioned that social and political conditions have much influence in moulding religious opinions, and we assume that the democratic spirit will rule the future. What kind of religious influence is Democracy adapted to exert? In what direction does the democratic current run? According to De Tocqueville, it runs in the direction of very general ideas, and therefore to Pantheism. The idea of the unity of the people as a whole, as one, preponderates, and this extends itself to the world, and to the universe.

51

God and the universe make one whole. This unity has charms for men living in democracies, and prepares them for Pantheistic beliefs. 'Among the different systems, by whose aid philosophy endeavours to explain the universe, I believe Pantheism to be one of those most fitted to seduce the human mind in democratic ages; and against it all who abide in their attachment to the true greatness of man, should struggle and combine.'

If these remarks of this very acute political observer are true, we may expect to see Pantheism enlarging its influence in Christendom as Democracy extends.

More and more all sovereigns and rulers are eager to learn what the wishes of their people are, and careful not to set themselves in direct opposition to them. Whether in the existing monarchies hereditary succession will give place to popular election, is not certain, though it seems probable; but all rulers, hereditary or elected, are made more and more to feel themselves the servants of the people.

This growth of Democracy serves to prepare the way of the Antichrist by making the popular will supreme, both as to the choice of the rulers and the nature and extent of their rule; and by giving legal expression to that will. When a people elects its legislators, the legislation will be what the majority of the voters demand.

If then, the belief become general, either that there is no God, the Lawgiver, or no expression of His will, which is authoritative, what principle shall determine the character and limitations of legislation? The only principle is that of the public good; whatever this demands, is right. If, for example, the law of marriage given in the Bible is set aside as without authority, what shall determine what the new law shall be? It must be what the welfare of society demands, and this is a matter of popular judgment (pages 254–255, 264–265. Original copyright 1889, republished in 1937 by Moody Press).

The original copyright of this book was 1898, when there was no evidence of popular democracy anywhere. Here we clearly recognize the spirit of the Gentile power structure dominated by the Roman spirit, the final Gentile superpower, the iron/clay kingdom.

The Babylonian World

Back to our question: Why was the Babylonian Empire considered the best and our modern democracy considered the worst form of government? Why did the

Why was the Babylonian Empire considered the best and our modern democracy considered the worst form of government?

seemingly brutal King Nebuchadnezzar represent the best kingdom? Verse 38 says: "Thou art this head of gold." There are many reasons, but we'll look at three.

First, the infrastructure of Babylon's government must have been excellent because it existed without a king for seven years. What happened to King Nebuchadnezzar? We read in Daniel 4:25: "They shall drive thee from men, and thy dwelling shall be with the beasts of the field, and they shall make thee to eat grass as oxen, and they shall wet thee with the dew of heaven, and seven times shall pass over thee, till thou know that the most High ruleth in the kingdom of men, and giveth it to whomsoever he will."

We heard about crises developing in the U.S. during the few minutes we were without a president after Kennedy was assassinated. This was repeated in a similar fashion when President Reagan was shot and wounded. Although the Washington government could work without a president for some time, the leadership concentration on one person is extremely important. Without that leader, it is impossible for the nation to function properly.

In Nebuchadnezzar's case, Babylon continued to be the leading world power during and after those seven years had expired. Nebuchadnezzar was restored to his power and rulership in Babylon.

Second, the Babylonian kingdom was superior to all others because God could directly interfere in the affairs of men through one person: King Nebuchadnezzar. In the end he humbled himself and recognized the truth of God's Word. Here is King

Nebuchadnezzar's testimony: "And at the end of the day I Nebuchadnezzar lifted up mine eyes unto heaven, and mine understanding returned unto me, and I blessed the most High, and I praised and honoured him that liveth for ever, whose dominion is an everlasting dominion, and his kingdom is from generation to generation" (Daniel 4:34).

Third, the Babylonian kingdom was great because God called the pagan-worshipping Gentile King Nebuchadnezzar his servant. Let us read the testimony in Jeremiah 27:6: "And now have I given all these lands into the hand of Nebuchadnezzar the king of Babylon, my servant; and the beasts of the field have I given him also to serve him." Why was the king God's servant? Because he did what he was instructed to do; he was humiliated but healed, debased but elevated. Today, all governments blatantly reject the God of Israel. This is the foundation upon which democracy is built: "We the people are in charge."

After Babylon

The two kingdoms following Babylon are described with only 24 words: "And after thee shall arise another kingdom inferior to thee, and another third kingdom of brass, which shall bear rule over all the earth" (Daniel 2:39).

Then comes the fourth kingdom. The final Gentile power structure is described in extensive detail and closer events are revealed later in the book of

Revelation. Let's read one verse: "The fourth kingdom shall be strong as iron: forasmuch as iron breaketh in pieces and subdueth all things: and as iron that breaketh all these, shall it break in pieces and bruise" (Daniel 2:40).

Some may say these kingdoms did not literally rule over all the earth. That is true. If we looked at a map, we would see that Babylon was relatively small. Only the southern region of Turkey belonged to Babylon. The border extended down to Egypt along the coastline and crossed areas of Saudi Arabia up to the Persian Gulf.

The expansion of the Persian Empire went further and included portions of Greece. While the Grecian Empire went past today's Pakistan, it also included several southeastern European countries. But the Roman Empire included all the Mediterranean countries and virtually all of Europe. However, we must emphasize that "Rome" does not refer only to a city, nor is the term limited to the country of Italy or even to the European continent. Rather, it refers to the entire Roman civilization, whose culture and law have changed the entire world and whose influence continues today. This also applies to Babylon, Media-Persia and Greece; thus the Bible's statement that these four Gentile power structures dominate the entire world is correct. Therefore, I must reject the description "to the then-known world." The Bible says "all the earth."

Three Out of Five Continents Are Roman

Of the world's five continents, only Africa and Asia are not completely European. But virtually all of Africa's 40 countries were former European colonies built on the principles of European cultures and laws.

This is also true to a lesser extent for Asia. At one time or another, much of the continent was divided into various European colonies. Therefore, Roman law is still the chief method of governing within most Asian nations. Thus, we see the fourth and final world empire literally encompass the world.

This will become even more obvious in the near future as the nucleus of Roman principles is reconstructed by the European Union.

The End of Gentile Power

What will happen to these four Gentile superpowers? We already have a partial answer in the recent devastation of Babylon (Iraq) by the US and Britain during their search for Saddam Hussein and his weapons of mass destruction. Thus, we realize that Babylon is still a reality, even though it no longer functions as the kingdom it was during Nebuchadnezzar's time. Babylon ceased to exist as an independent nation in 570 B.C. and then Media-Persia took over. That empire was defeated by Greece and then Rome later defeated Greece.

However, we must not overlook that they have to exist as nations in order to be destroyed. Scripture says: "Thou sawest till that a stone was cut out without hands, which smote the image upon his feet that were of iron and clay, and brake them to pieces. Then was the iron, the clay, the brass, the silver, and the gold, broken to pieces together, and became like the chaff of the summer threshingfloors; and the wind carried them away, that no place was found for them: and the stone that smote the image became a great mountain, and filled the whole earth" (Daniel 2:34–35). The destruction will begin with the iron-clay empire and then all the others will collapse on top of it.

The Four-Fold Empire Is Still Alive

In recent years these four former world empires became involved in military conflicts. Iraq [Babylon] and Iran [Persia] fought an eight-year war that resulted in more than a million casualties on each side. In the 1970s Greece fought with Turkey over the island of Cyprus. For all practical purposes, the last two Iraq/US conflicts were between Babylon and Rome, the first and the last Gentile superpowers. Although Europe overwhelmingly opposed this last war, we cannot deny that the United States is a product of Europe and therefore qualifies as being part of the fourth Gentile superpower: the iron-clay kingdom. Besides, this last iron-clay empire is not limited to Europe but it is global. This political, economic, financial and religious system "shall bear rule over all the earth." Apparently no country is exempt.

The Iron-Clay Mixture

Special focus should be directed to the feet of this great image as being a mixture of two non-binding materials: "whereas thou sawest the feet and toes, part of potters' clay, and part of iron, the kingdom shall be divided; but there shall be in it of the strength of the iron, forasmuch as thou sawest the iron mixed with miry clay. And as the toes of the feet were part of iron, and part of clay, so the kingdom shall be partly strong, and partly bro-

Rome is not limited to a city, nor is it limited to the country of Italy or even to the European continent.

ken. And whereas thou sawest iron mixed with miry clay, they shall mingle themselves with the seed of men: but they shall not cleave one to another, even as iron is not mixed with clay" (Daniel 2:41–43). That's different from all the other kingdoms.

There was no mixing with the gold, silver and brass empires, but the mixing is specifically emphasized with the last one. Thus, the question immediately arises: Whom does the clay represent?

Jewish Mixture with the Nations

We know the iron is the Roman power structure. I believe the answer to our question about the clay is found in the middle of verse 43: "they shall mingle themselves with the seed of men." The "they" referred to in this verse is the clay. Isaiah 64:8

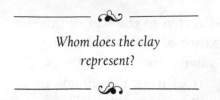

Whom does the clay represent?

answers: "But now, O LORD, thou art our father, we are the clay, and thou our potter; and we all are the work of thy hand." The Lord confirms this in Jeremiah 18:6: "O house of Israel, cannot I do with you as this potter? saith the LORD. Behold, as the clay is in the potter's hand, so are ye in mine hand, O house of Israel."

When we read Israel's history we realize the Jews do indeed represent the clay because they were able to adapt themselves to any country in which they lived. Although the Jews have been discriminated against and often have been persecuted and even killed, they have lived among other people without becoming part of them: "they shall not cleave one to another, even as iron is not mixed with clay."

Christians: A Separate Nation

Scripture says that as believers we are in the world but we are not to be of the world. The Apostle Paul made this clear in 2 Corinthians 6:17: "Wherefore come out from among them, and be ye separate, saith the Lord, and touch not the unclean thing; and I will receive you." This biblical teaching seems almost impossible for some Christians to grasp. We like to have it both ways: the flag in one hand and the cross in the other. But these two things have nothing to do with each other. The flag represents a political entity under the jurisdiction of the prince of darkness. The cross, on the other hand, divides us from this world; we just can't have it both ways.

That doesn't mean we are to forsake our nation, belittle our leaders or despise our government. We are instructed to honor those to whom honor is due, respect the authorities and abide by the laws of the land. Unfortunately, today's Christianity, especially in the U.S.A., has been politicized to such an extent that it is in danger of being swallowed up through an intermingling with the world.

During a recent prophecy conference I shared this fact with the audience, particularly relating to the political slogan: "We are the greatest nation in the world." There was silence. At the end of my message I went to the book table, where a woman approached me and said, "I asked my husband to shoot you." Of course she was kidding but keep in mind that these people love the prophetic Word and invest their time and money in attending such conferences; yet, as this example shows, many are in total darkness as far as the political identities of the nations are concerned.

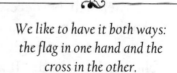

We like to have it both ways: the flag in one hand and the cross in the other.

Recently I noticed that every article in one Christian publication mentioned politics. Apparently, politics can be more important than the Bible to some people.

Segregation or Integration?

What about the Jews? When the Jews were presented with a choice of releasing Barabbas or Jesus, they chose Barabbas and said: "We have no king but Caesar." Thus, they publicly admitted their desire to be subject to international law, in this case to Caesar of Rome.

Furthermore, the declaration of Israel's independence includes this statement: "It is moreover the self-evident right of the Jewish people to be a nation as all other nations in its own sovereign state." Another paragraph reads, "We appeal to the United Nations to assist the Jewish people in the building of its state to admit Israel into the family of nations." That is Israel's greatest tragedy: rejecting its special calling to be separate from the nations of the world and to be holy unto the Lord.

Israel will be deceived by the Antichrist just as prophesied, not because of any outside force but because it knowingly and intentionally made that choice. Jesus said: "If another shall come in his own name, him ye will receive" (John 5:43).

A Holy Nation

The moment we were born again to a living hope, we became separated from the world according to God's authority. The Apostle Peter wrote: "But ye are a chosen generation, a royal priesthood, an holy nation, a peculiar people; that ye should shew forth the praises of him who hath called you out of darkness into his marvellous light" (1 Peter 2:9). This is a serious warning to Christians. We are different, we are "peculiar," we are not of this world. What a tragedy that countless Christians reject this high calling and make this world their home, their hope and their future.

Israel's Destiny

Israel's end will be decided by an act of grace as recorded in Daniel 2:44–45: "And in

What a tragedy that countless Christians reject this high calling and make this world their home.

the days of these kings shall the God of heaven set up a kingdom, which shall never be destroyed: and the kingdom shall not be left to other people, but it shall break in pieces and consume all these kingdoms, and it shall stand for ever. Forasmuch as thou sawest that the stone was cut out of the mountain without hands, and that it brake in pieces the iron, the brass, the clay, the silver, and the gold; the great God hath made known to the king what shall come to pass hereafter: and the dream is certain, and the interpretation thereof sure." The entire global system, which includes more than 200 countries, has no future, but the kingdom God has established shall stand forever!

Chapter 3

GLOBAL RELIGION

"Nebuchadnezzar the king made an image of gold, whose height was threescore cubits and the breadth thereof six cubits: he set it up in the plain of Dura, in the province of Babylon" (Daniel 3:1).

The Image of the Nations

King Nebuchadnezzar, leader of Babylon's golden kingdom, tried to establish a global religion that was visibly manifested by the manufacturing of a golden image. To get a picture of this remarkable work of art, we must understand that 66 cubits is approximately the height of an eight-story building. It must have been very expensive because the Bible says the image was made of gold. Why gold? The Babylonian kingdom was considered the "golden" kingdom. Nebuchadnezzar was told, "Thou art this head of gold."

We can sense Nebuchadnezzar's self-centeredness. He was number one; he was the gold; and he was the greatest. Although he had just confessed, "Of a truth it is, that your God is a God of gods and a Lord of kings, and a revealer of secrets" (Daniel 2:47), he apparently did not recognize the God of Israel. Nebuchadnezzar experienced God's power when Daniel interpreted his dream, but he did not see or hear Him. Therefore, Nebuchadnezzar's statement of faith, "Your God is a God of gods," was based on a visible experience, not on a spiritual reality.

Nebuchadnezzar's intention is recorded in verses 2–3, where we read that he gathered together the leaders of the world: "Then Nebuchadnezzar the king sent to gather together the princes, the governors, and the captains, the judges, the treasurers, the counsellors, the sheriffs, and all the rulers of the provinces, to come to the dedication of the image which

Nebuchadnezzar the king had set up. Then the princes, the governors, and captains, the judges, the treasurers, the counsellors, the sheriffs, and all the rulers of the provinces, were gathered together unto the dedication of the image that Nebuchadnezzar the king had set up; and they stood before the image that Nebuchadnezzar had set up" (verse 3).

United Religion

The purpose of this image is revealed next: "Then an herald cried aloud, To you it is commanded, O people, nations, and languages, that at what time ye hear the sound of the cornet, flute, harp, sackbut, psaltery, dulcimer, and all kinds of musick, ye fall down and worship the golden image that Nebuchadnezzar the king hath set up: And whoso falleth not down and worshippeth shall the same hour be cast into the midst of a burning fiery furnace" (verses 4–6).

A one-world political system already existed and was led by Nebuchadnezzar. Such leadership must have included military power and a good economy; otherwise, he would not have been able to build such an impressive image. The communication system must also have functioned well because when all of the rulers under his authority were instructed to come, they came. But one thing was lacking: a united religion!

Conflicting Religions

One look at the newspaper is all we need to realize that religion is one of the major components of disunity, conflict and war.

This became a vivid reality during my recent visit to India. The media broadcasted daily reports about the clashes between the Hindus and the Muslims that caused many casualties. Christians are also under pressure. During a private conversation with some of the church leaders, we discussed the percentage of Christians in that particular city. One brother said that region was approximately 20 percent Christian. Another added that there were many more. A third man said, "Let's keep it [the percentage] low so we do not become a cause of concern to our Hindu government." Then I heard first-hand about certain activities that made it clear that Christians in India are being oppressed.

When we look at the Middle East, we see extreme violence, especially against the Jewish state of Israel. In general, Islam is the source of today's feared terrorist activities the world over. Religion, therefore, is extremely important for a nation, or in this case, a world empire, to function properly.

The Russian-led communist empire didn't last too long because it openly rejected and even persecuted religions. But, religion is an integral part of any civilized society and is just as necessary as a political philosophy, a military force and a financial system.

Not surprisingly, the devil uses religion to deceive

the world. Thus, religion and commerce will ultimately be integrated to such an extent that one won't exist without the other: "He had power to give life unto the image of the beast, that the image of the beast should both speak, and cause that as many as would not worship the image of the beast should be killed. And he causeth all, both small and great, rich and poor, free and bond, to receive a mark in their right hand, or in their foreheads: And that no man might buy or sell, save he that had the mark, or the name of the beast, or the number of his name" (Revelation 13:15–17).

The devil uses religion to deceive the world.

Babylon Religion

A religious demonstration was understandably necessary in order to manifest unity and solidify the Babylonian world empire: "United we stand, divided we fall." Scripture assigns a numeric value to this ultimate leader: "and his number is Six hundred threescore and six" (Revelation 13:18) — that is, 666. It is not coincidental that the image Nebuchadnezzar built was 60 cubits high by 6 cubits wide. Furthermore, verse 5 lists six musical instruments used to call the nations to worship: cornet, flute, harp, sackbut, psaltery, and dulcimer.

These six instruments were the basis of the very first international religious music festival, designed to produce a unified spirit that would cause everyone to worship this man-made image.

Religious Church Music

This reminds me of today's church music, which has the same sound and effect it did during Nebuchadnezzar's time and can be played for pleasure and entertainment to any group of people. That is why I object to modern music in a church setting. When the borders that separate Christian and secular music are erased, then I must warn against it.

Of course, it is difficult to judge what type of music can be considered godly because culture, tradition and taste must be considered. The younger generation seems to like contemporary music. But I have never heard any young, born-again believer object to singing such classic hymns as "Amazing Grace," "At the Cross," or "Blessed Assurance." If certain types of music are used in services that are found to be objectionable to those in attendance, then I don't think such music should be used as a call to worship. If certain music causes division, then we have reason to exercise caution.

I often hear people say we need to use modern music in order to reach our youth. That may very well be true, but my recent experience proved just the opposite. Midnight Call's international headquarters is located in Zurich, Switzerland. Each year it sponsors an annual Easter conference. I did not hear one modern song during the entire conference yet I was quite surprised to see that the younger people out-numbered the older ones in the 1,000-plus seat auditorium. Apparently, the brethren did not see a need for drums, rock-and-roll singers or Christian artists in order to attract the younger people.

Global Worship

What happened when the music played before the golden image? "All the people, the nations, and the languages, fell down and worshipped the golden image that Nebuchadnezzar the king had set up" (Daniel 3:7). But there was an exception: three Jewish men refused to participate: "Wherefore at that time certain Chaldeans came near, and accused the Jews" (Daniel 3:8).

Unger's Bible Dictionary defines the "Chaldeans" this way:

> Because of their proficiency in the science of astronomy and their skillful practice of astrology, the Chaldeans became a special caste of astrologers. In this sense the word is used in the book of Daniel (2:2, 10; 4:7, etc.). The explanation of this specialized name is easily understood. From 625 B.C. onward the Chaldeans held complete sway in Babylonia. The city of Babylon was their capital and was the very center of intellectual life in all western Asia. This intellectual activity was especially employed in the study of the stars, both scientific and as a means of divination. Astronomy and astrology were both sought after in the land. Hence

> Babylon became famous as the home of all sorts of magicians, sorcerers, diviners and other occultists. As scientists the Chaldeans founded the exact science of astronomy.
>
> *-Moody Press*, Pg. 187

These Chaldeans went before the king and accused the Jews: "There are certain Jews whom thou hast set over the affairs of the province of Babylon, Shadrach, Meshach, and Abednego; these men, O king, have not regarded thee: they serve not thy gods, nor worship the golden image which thou hast set up" (Daniel 3:12). The golden image Nebuchadnezzar had built in the Babylonian province was created to unify all religions. All people had to become equal; therefore, only one god and one type of worship was accepted.

Those who believe in Jesus Christ during the Great Tribulation will refuse to worship the image of the beast.

We have to keep this fact in mind because Babylon is the first Gentile superpower and the last Gentile superpower is called "Mystery Babylon, the great, the mother of harlots and abominations of the earth" (Revelation 17:5).

According to God's Word, all religions will ultimately unite under one authority; otherwise, prophecy cannot be fulfilled. For example, Revelation 13:8 says this about the Antichrist: "And all that dwell upon the earth shall worship him." In this case, the Bible identifies a remnant: "whose names are not written in the book of life of the Lamb slain from the foundation of the world." Those who believe in Jesus Christ during the Great Tribulation will refuse to worship the image of the beast.

The Three Believers

How did King Nebuchadnezzar react to the three Jewish men who defied the government? "Then Nebuchadnezzar in his rage and fury commanded to bring Shadrach, Meshach, and Abednego. Then they brought these men before the king" (Daniel 3:13).

At first, however, when they stood before Nebuchadnezzar, he camouflaged his "rage and fury" and tried to use a little friendly diplomatic persuasion. "Nebuchadnezzar spake and said unto them, Is it true, O Shadrach, Meshach, and Abednego, do not ye serve my gods, nor worship the golden image which I have set up? Now if ye be ready that at what time ye hear the sound of the cornet, flute, harp, sackbut, psaltery, and dulcimer, and all kinds of musick, ye fall down and worship the image which I have made; well: but if ye worship not, ye shall be cast the same hour into the midst of a burning fiery furnace; and who is that God that shall deliver you out of my hands?" (verses 14–15). That sounds reasonable. The king was going to give the Jews another chance. Actually, he couldn't believe anyone would oppose this ecumenical worship ceremony. He asked: "Is it true, O Shadrach, Meshach, and Abednego do not ye serve my gods, nor worship the golden image which I have set up?" In modern English, we would say, "Come on! You can't be serious. This is for the good of our nation. You are in a great position. Don't rebel against my authority. Have you forgotten that God has ordained me as the leader of the world? Don't you remember that your friend Daniel prophesied that I, the king, am the head of gold? Be reasonable! Cooperate and compromise just a little. This won't hurt you and it will preserve unity in my kingdom!"

How did the three men answer? "If it be so, our God whom we serve is able to deliver us from the burning fiery furnace, and he will deliver us out of thine hand, O king. But if not, be it known unto thee, O king, that we will not serve thy gods, nor worship the golden image which thou hast set up" (verses 17–18).

Four Men in the Furnace

Nebuchadnezzar wanted these three men eliminated immediately: "Then was Nebuchadnezzar full of fury, and the form of his visage was changed against Shadrach, Meshach, and Abednego: therefore he spake, and commanded that they should heat the furnace one seven times more than it was wont to be heated. And he commanded the most mighty men that were in his army to bind Shadrach, Meshach, and Abednego, and to cast them into the burning fiery furnace. Then these men were bound in their coats, their hosen, and their hats, and their other garments, and were cast into the midst of the burning fiery furnace. Therefore because the king's commandment was urgent, and the furnace exceeding hot, the flame of the fire slew those men that took up Shadrach, Meshach, and Abednego. And these three men, Shadrach, Meshach, and Abednego, fell down bound into the midst of the burning fiery furnace" (Daniel 3:19–23).

Something remarkable happened after the men were thrown into the furnace: "Nebuchadnezzar the king was astonied, and rose up in haste, and spake, and said unto his counsellors, Did not we cast three men bound into the midst of the fire? They answered and said unto the king, True, O king. He answered and said, Lo, I see four men loose, walking in the midst of the fire, and they have no hurt; and the form of the fourth is like the Son of God" (verses 24–25).

What began as furious rage ended in humility. King Nebuchadnezzar testified of the living God: "Then Nebuchadnezzar came near to the mouth of the burning fiery furnace, and spake, and said, Shadrach, Meshach, and Abednego, ye servants of the most high God, come forth, and come hither. Then Shadrach, Meshach, and Abednego, came forth of the midst of the fire. And the princes, governors, and captains, and the king's counsellors, being gathered together, saw these men, upon whose bodies the fire had no power, nor was an hair of their head singed, neither were their coats changed, nor the smell of fire had passed on them" (verses 26–27).

Nebuchadnezzar the Missionary

As a result, Nebuchadnezzar experienced another conversion: "Then Nebuchadnezzar spake, and said, Blessed be the God of Shadrach, Meshach, and Abednego, who hath sent his angel, and delivered his servants that trusted in him, and have changed the king's word, and yielded their bodies, that they might not serve nor worship any god, except their own God. Therefore I make a decree, That every people, nation, and language, which speak any thing amiss against the God of Shadrach, Meshach, and Abednego, shall be cut in pieces, and their houses shall be made a dunghill: because there is no other God that can deliver after this sort. Then the king promoted Shadrach, Meshach, and Abednego, in the province of Babylon" (verses 28–30). Instead of destroying the Jewish men, he threatened to destroy anyone who uttered a word against the God of Israel. The living God humbled the first ruler of the first Gentile world empire.

The last king, "Mystery Babylon," the Antichrist and his servants, will try to destroy the Jewish people but he, too, will fail. His end is described in Revelation 20:10: "And the devil that deceived them was cast into the lake of fire and brimstone, where the beast and the false prophet are, and shall be tormented day and night for ever and ever."

An Anti-Israel World

We live under the auspices of the iron empire today. Again the Jews are different; they don't follow in the footsteps of the rest of the world. Although Israel would like to become an equal member of the family of nations, it still hasn't been accepted. The world already has decided against the Jews

Not one nation supports Israel's right to the Promised Land as defined in Scripture — from the Euphrates River to the river of Egypt.

and the land of Israel. I cannot repeat it often enough: No nation supports Israel's right to the Promised Land as defined in Scripture — from the Euphrates River to the river of Egypt. The leaders of every nation agree with the mandates of the prince of darkness in believing that Israel must not be allowed to fully possess the land God gave to them. They try to nullify the eternal written Word of God. But the end for them will be the same as prophesied by King Nebuchadnezzar in his declaration: "Therefore I make a decree, That every people, nation, and language, which speak any thing amiss against the God of Shadrach, Meshach, and Abednego, shall be cut in pieces, and their houses shall be made a dunghill: because there is no other God that can deliver after this sort" (Daniel 3:29).

Chapter 4

Nebuchadnezzar's Testimony

"Nebuchadnezzar the king, unto all people, nations, and languages, that dwell in all the earth; Peace be multiplied unto you. I thought it good to shew the signs and wonders that the high God hath wrought toward me. How great are his signs! And how mighty are his wonders! His kingdom is an everlasting kingdom, and his dominion is from generation to generation" (Daniel 4:1–3).

This amazing testimony comes from a Gentile world ruler about the God of heaven! Nebuchadnezzar was confronted with the God of Israel when Daniel interpreted his first dream about the nations of the world. Then he had an encounter with four men in a burning furnace. This man, this king, not only experienced miracles but he also believed and ultimately gave God the honor and the glory. That is why he is called "the head of gold."

Before we proceed, it is important to point out that Nebuchadnezzar's testimony is unique among the Gentile rulers: "Now I Nebuchadnezzar praise and extol and honour the King of heaven, all whose works are truth, and his ways judgment: and those that walk in pride he is able to abase" (Daniel 4:37). He was fully aware that he had experienced an encounter with the living God.

Furthermore, this chapter shows the entire Gentile structure throughout history. The God of heaven and earth "ruleth in the kingdom of men and giveth it to whomsoever he will, and setteth up over it the basest of men" (verse 17).

Also important is that Nebuchadnezzar addressed all people, nations and languages. Some may say the kingdom of Babylon was rather small; it stretched from Egypt in the west and along the Mediterranean to the south of Turkey, across to the Arabian Sea and back to the Red Sea. Only a small part of Africa, a little bit of Asia and Europe weren't even touched by its borders. However, we must not overlook that all humanity falls into this four-fold kingdom: Babylon, Media-Persia, Greece and Rome. No kingdoms have influenced the world as extensively as these four. The fourth one in particular, Rome, has spread its influence throughout the entire world. The Bible only identifies three continents: Asia, Africa and Europe. For all practical purposes, America and Australia are extensions of the fourth world empire: Rome (Europe). If we stick to what the text says, which is "all people" and "all the earth," then we can't go wrong, even though the people in Europe, most of Africa and the majority of Asia heard nothing about Nebuchadnezzar.

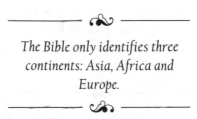

The Bible only identifies three continents: Asia, Africa and Europe.

The Dream

Nebuchadnezzar had a strange dream: "I saw a dream which made me afraid, and the thoughts upon my bed and the visions of my head troubled me" (verse 5). He asked his advisors for an interpretation: "Then came in the magicians, the astrologers, the Chaldeans, and the soothsayers: and I told the dream before them; but they did not make known unto me the interpretation thereof" (verse 7). Naturally, they did not have an answer.

Hidden Future

Even today, the prognosticators, political scientists,

and economists try — and fail — to forecast the future. The most they can do is learn from the past and establish a hypothesis of what we might expect in the future.

Automobiles, for example, are being improved upon each year so we can expect — even predict — that in five years they will be even more efficient, better built and have greater capability than the vehicles built today. But that represents the extent of our ability to know what's going to happen in the future. No one can predict when the next airplane will go down, what airline or the type of plane it will be, the number of casualties, or the location of the crash. We simply don't know.

Although Daniel faithfully served King Nebuchadnezzar, he never became integrated into Babylonian society but remained a Jew.

The Gentile Tree

"But at the last Daniel came in before me, whose name was Belteshazzar, according to the name of my god, and in whom is the spirit of the holy gods: and before him I told the dream" (verse 8). It is significant that Nebuchadnezzar acknowledged Daniel by his proper name. This further testifies that although Daniel faithfully served King Nebuchadnezzar, he never became integrated into Babylonian society, but remained a Jew.

Here is the dream: "Thus were the visions of mine

head in my bed; I saw, and behold a tree in the midst of the earth, and the height thereof was great. The tree grew, and was strong, and the height thereof reached unto heaven, and the sight thereof to the end of all the earth: The leaves thereof were fair, and the fruit thereof much, and in it was meat for all: the beasts of the field had shadow under it, and the fowls of the heaven dwelt in the boughs thereof, and all flesh was fed of it. I saw in the visions of my head upon my bed, and, behold, a watcher and an holy one came down from heaven; He cried aloud, and said thus, Hew down the tree, and cut off his branches, shake off his leaves, and scatter his fruit: let the beasts get away from under it, and the fowls from his branches: Nevertheless leave the stump of his roots in the earth, even with a band of iron and brass, in the tender grass of the field; and let it be wet with the dew of heaven, and let his portion be with the beasts in the grass of the earth: Let his heart be changed from man's, and let a beast's heart be given unto him; and let seven times pass over him. This matter is by the decree of the watchers, and the demand by the word of the holy ones: to the intent that the living may know that the most High ruleth in the kingdom of men, and giveth it to whomsoever he will, and setteth up over it the basest of men" (verses 10-17).

Again, Nebuchadnezzar acknowledged the God of Israel, the God who "changeth the times and the seasons, he removeth kings, and setteth up kings" (Daniel 2:21).

This same God is in charge today, which is why Scripture admonishes believers to obey their respective governments: "Let every soul be subject unto the higher powers. For there is no power but of God: the powers that be are ordained of God. Whosoever therefore resisteth the power, resisteth the ordinance of God: and they that resist shall receive to themselves damnation" (Romans 13:1–2). That instruction is not limited to governments we agree with; it includes all governments in all time

The Interpretation

"Then Daniel, whose name was Belteshazzar, was astonied for one hour, and his thoughts troubled him. The king spake, and said, Belteshazzar, let not the dream, or the interpretation thereof, trouble thee. Belteshazzar answered and said, My lord, the dream be to them that hate thee, and the interpretation thereof to thine enemies" (verse 19). This reveals the dedication with which Daniel served the king. He easily could have said: "You had it coming," but he humbly announced that he wished this dream to be for his enemies, not his lord.

Daniel explained that the tree symbolized the king of Babylon. Then verse 22 says: "It is thou, O king, that art grown and become strong: for thy greatness is grown, and reacheth unto heaven, and thy dominion to the end of the earth." Notice the direction here is vertical, as indicated by the phrase "unto heaven," and horizontal, as denoted by the phrase "to the end of the earth." That reinforces Nebuchadnezzar's uniqueness: He not only had a far-reaching influence on earth; he also had contact with God "unto heaven."

Next comes the judgment: "they shall drive thee from men, and thy dwelling shall be with the beasts of the field, and they shall make thee to eat grass as oxen, and they shall wet thee with the dew of heaven, and seven times shall pass over thee, till thou know that the most High ruleth in the kingdom of men, and giveth it to whomsoever he will" (verse 25). Daniel again confronted Nebuchadnezzar with the reality of the God who "giveth it to whomsoever he will."

Pride Comes Before the Fall

A year had passed when judgment came: "The king spake, and said, Is not this great Babylon, that I have built for the house of the kingdom by the might of my power, and for the honour of my majesty? While the word was in the king's mouth, there fell a voice from heaven, saying, O king Nebuchadnezzar, to thee it is spoken; The kingdom is departed from thee" (verses 30–31). In spite of his experiences and testimony, Nebuchadnezzar could not escape that he was the great king — the greatest, the head of gold: "I have built...by the might of my power...for the honor of my majesty."

Seven Prophetic Years

The great King Nebuchadnezzar of the first Gentile

superpower was debased to the level of an animal: "The same hour was the thing fulfilled upon Nebuchadnezzar: and he was driven from men, and did eat grass as oxen, and his body was wet with the dew of heaven, till his hairs were grown like eagles' feathers, and his nails like birds' claws" (verse 33).

After the seven years, "And at the end of the days I Nebuchadnezzar lifted up mine eyes unto heaven, and mine understanding returned unto me, and I blessed the most High, and I praised and honoured him that liveth for ever, whose dominion is an everlasting dominion, and his kingdom is from generation to generation" (verse 34).

This prophetically points to the coming seven-year Tribulation that will occur during the time of "Mystery Babylon," the final Gentile empire. Man will then be reduced to the level of animals, voluntarily worshipping a man as God and accepting his total control. They will fight against the God of heaven, as we learn in Revelation 9:20–21. "And the rest of the men which were not killed by these plagues yet repented not of the works of their hands, that they should not worship devils, and idols of gold, and silver, and brass, and stone, and of wood: which neither can see, nor hear, nor walk: Neither repented they of their murders, nor of their sorceries, nor of their fornication, nor of their thefts."

Nebuchadnezzar did change; in the next chapter, Daniel documents the king's conversion: "O thou king, the most high God gave Nebuchadnezzar thy father a kingdom, and majesty, and glory, and honour: And for the majesty that he gave him, all people, nations, and languages, trembled and feared before him: whom he would he slew; and whom he would he kept alive; and whom he would he set up; and whom he would he put down. But when his heart was lifted up, and his mind hardened in pride, he was deposed from his kingly throne, and they took his glory from him: And he was driven from the sons of men; and his heart was made like the beasts, and his dwelling was with the wild asses: they fed him with grass like oxen, and his body was wet with the dew of heaven; till he knew that the most high God ruled in the kingdom of men, and that he appointeth over it whomsoever he will" (Daniel 5:18–21).

Nebuchadnezzar's Testimony

Notice how Nebuchadnezzar glorified God with his testimony. "At the same time my reason returned unto me; and for the glory of my kingdom, mine honour and brightness returned unto me; and my counsellors and my lords sought unto me; and I was established in my kingdom, and excellent majesty was added unto me. Now I Nebuchadnezzar praise and extol and honour the King of heaven, all whose works are truth, and his ways judgment: and those that walk in pride he is able to abase" (Daniel 4:36–37).

The Best and the Worst

Now we should understand that Nebuchadnezzar was called "the head of gold," which represented the best type of government. The worst type of government was represented by the iron-clay mixture, the category in which our democratic form of government can be classified. We, not God, are in charge; we, not God, establish our laws; we, not God, plan our futures and leave God out of those plans. I am reminded of a statement British politician Winston Churchill once made: "Democracy is the worst form of government but it is the best we have."

"Democracy is the worst form of government but it is the best we have."

Some people may point out that many within our government are born-again Christians. That certainly doesn't compare with the pagan Nebuchadnezzar. Of course, there are individual politicians who happen to be Christians; however, that doesn't define the government — nor are any of these Christian individuals actually in charge. They are where they are because the people put them there. The majority elects the leaders and since the majority of people are evil, it stands to reason that nothing but evil will therefore come out of our government.

Chapter 5

WEIGHED AND FOUND WANTING

"Belshazzar the king made a great feast to a thousand of his lords, and drank wine before the thousand. Belshazzar, whiles he tasted the wine, commanded to bring the golden and silver vessels which his father Nebuchadnezzar had taken out of the temple which was in Jerusalem; that the king, and his princes, his wives, and his concubines, might drink therein. Then they brought the golden vessels that were taken out of the temple of the house of God which was at Jerusalem; and the king, and his princes, his wives, and his concubines, drank in them. They drank wine, and praised the gods of gold, and of silver, of brass, of iron, of wood, and of stone "
(Daniel 5:1–4).

Chapter 5 of Daniel graphically describes the glory and downfall of the world's greatest Gentile nation. When we study the story of Belshazzar, which climaxes with the handwriting on the wall, we must keep in mind that Babylon was destined to be replaced. According to the image Daniel described in Chapter 2, Babylon was the kingdom of gold. Next came the kingdom of silver, the Media-Persian Empire. Regardless of Belshazzar's behavior, the prophetic Word's call for Babylon's end would be fulfilled. Nevertheless, the person in charge was responsible for his actions.

Verses 3–4 reveal the horrendous mistakes King Belshazzar made: "Then they brought the golden vessels that were taken out of the temple of the house of God which was at Jerusalem; and the king, and his princes, his wives, and his concubines, drank in them. They drank wine, and praised the gods of gold, and of silver, of brass, of iron, of wood, and of stone" (Daniel 5:3–4). Notice the words "temple," "house of God," and "Jerusalem." That is typical of the spirit of Babel: mixing the holy with the unholy.

Mystery Babylon at Work Today

No wonder the endtime Gentile superpower is called "Mystery Babylon." Revelation 18:3 explains why: "For all nations have drunk of the wine of the wrath of her fornication, and the kings of the earth have committed fornication with her, and the merchants of the earth are waxed rich through the abundance of her delicacies." In this context, fornication refers to religion, which is on the throne again today. Atheism received its knockout punch with the fall of the Soviet Union. Religion has become an integral part of the polit-ical and economic sys-tem, which accurately aligns itself with the previously quoted Scripture.

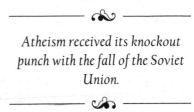

Atheism received its knockout punch with the fall of the Soviet Union.

For example, no American politician would dare suggest removing the phrase "In God We Trust" from our currency because its sentiment is generic enough to please all religions. It has also become a popular motto within the fields of business and politics.

In contrast, the word "God" has been left out of the European Union's constitution. But no one would dare suggest removing the 12 stars that form a circle, symbolizing Maryology, from their flag, currency, and other such materials. Thus, in this case as well, the mixture of politics, business and religion amplifies the spirit of Babylon in all establishments.

The Writing on the Wall

Apparently Belshazzar had forgotten about Daniel, the Jew who had previously interpreted dreams and visions for Nebuchadnezzar. But suddenly, "In the same hour came forth fingers of a man's hand, and wrote over against the candlestick upon the plaister of the wall of the king's palace: and the king saw the part of the hand that wrote" (verse 5). Belshazzar was beside himself when the handwriting appeared on the wall. The astrologers, soothsayers and Chaldeans could not help. The situation grew desperate; Belshazzar didn't know what to do. He trembled as he waited for that which was to come. Suddenly a woman appeared: "Now the queen, by reason of the words of the king and his lords, came into the banquet house: and the queen spake and said, O king, live for ever: let not thy thoughts trouble thee, nor let thy countenance be changed: There is a man in thy kingdom, in whom is the spirit of the holy gods; and in the days of thy father light and understanding and wisdom, like the wisdom of the gods, was found in him; whom the king Nebuchadnezzar thy father, the king, I say, thy father, made master of the magicians, astrologers, Chaldeans, and soothsayers. Forasmuch as an excellent spirit, and knowledge, and understanding, interpreting of dreams, and shewing of hard sentences, and dissolving of doubts, were found in the same Daniel, whom the king named Belteshazzar: now let Daniel be called, and he will shew the interpretation" (verses 10–12).

This is typical behavior of a man who has forgotten the reality of the living God. Belshazzar and his people knew about Daniel, but they had apparently replaced worship of God with worship of idols; subsequently, Daniel became the last resort in the king's quest for the simple truth.

The queen's instructions were accepted: "Then was

Daniel brought in before the king. And the king spake and said unto Daniel, Art thou that Daniel, which art of the children of the captivity of Judah, whom the king my father brought out of Jewry? I have even heard of thee, that the spirit of the gods is in thee, and that light and understanding and excellent wisdom is found in thee. And now the wise men, the astrologers, have been brought in before me, that they should read this writing, and make known unto me the interpretation thereof: but they could not shew the interpretation of the thing: And I have heard of thee, that thou canst make interpretations, and dissolve doubts: now if thou canst read the writing, and make known to me the interpretation thereof, thou shalt be clothed with scarlet, and have a chain of gold about thy neck, and shalt be the third ruler in the kingdom" (verses 13–16).

"I Will Read the Writing"

It is significant to point out Daniel's courage and his assurance in the God of Israel: "Then Daniel answered and said before the king, Let thy gifts be to thyself, and give thy rewards to another; yet I will read the writing unto the king, and make known to him the interpretation" (verse 17). Daniel was fearless and one can sense the disdain he felt for this corrupt King Belshazzar. He even rejected the gifts the king offered him. Daniel brought this king a message of judgment that would lead to condemnation. In Nebuchadnezzar's case, he had brought a message of judgment that led to salvation.

Notice the different words he used: "I will read the writing." When he had been brought before King Nebuchadnezzar, he had said: "there is a God in heaven that revealeth secrets" (Daniel 2:28). An introduction to the God of Israel was not necessary with Belshazzar because he had indulged in Babylon's success and refused to humble himself before the God of heaven.

Judgment Leads to Condemnation

Daniel knew about the hardness of Belshazzar's heart. He explained what had happened to Nebuchadnezzar: "O thou king, the most high God gave Nebuchadnezzar thy father a kingdom, and majesty, and glory, and honour: And for the majesty that he gave him, all people, nations, and languages, trembled and feared before him: whom he would he slew; and whom he would he kept alive; and whom he would he set up; and whom he would he put down. But when his heart was lifted up, and his mind hardened in pride, he was deposed from his kingly throne, and they took his glory from him. And he was driven from the sons of men; and his heart was made like the beasts, and his dwelling was with the wild asses: they fed him with grass like oxen, and his body was wet with the dew of heaven; till he knew that the most high God ruled in the kingdom of men, and that he appointeth over it whomsoever he will" (Daniel 5:18–21).

Next came the thunderous judgment: "And thou his son, O Belshazzar, hast not humbled thine heart, though thou knewest all this; But hast lifted up thyself against the Lord of heaven; and they have brought the vessels of his house before thee, and thou, and thy lords, thy wives, and thy concubines, have drunk wine in them; and thou hast praised the gods of silver, and gold, of brass, iron, wood, and stone, which see not, nor hear, nor know: and the God in whose hand thy breath is, and whose are all thy ways, hast thou not glorified: Then was the part of the hand sent from him; and this writing was written" (verse 22–24).

Belshazzar's offense was his pride. He had the knowledge, but he did not humble himself. He allowed the use of the holy vessels to honor man-made idols, exhibiting the epitome of blasphemy.

"Thou Art Weighed...and Art Found Wanting"

Next Daniel made the judgment known: "And this is the writing that was written, MENE, MENE, TEKEL, UPHARSIN. This is the interpretation of the thing: MENE; God hath numbered thy kingdom, and finished it. TEKEL; Thou art weighed in the balances, and art found wanting. PERES; Thy kingdom is divided, and given to the Medes and Persians" (verses 25–28). What now? Belshazzar showed no sign of repentance, he didn't ask for forgiveness, and he showed no humility; his heart was hardened to the point of no return.

We read about Belshazzar's fate in Daniel 5:30: "In that night was Belshazzar the king of the Chaldeans slain." Babylon was judged because it violated God's holy instruments by using them in worship of their own gods. Regarding Babylon's judgment, Jeremiah wrote: "for his device is against Babylon, to destroy it; because it is the vengeance of the LORD, the vengeance of his temple" (Jeremiah 51:11).

Final Warning?

God still speaks through His Word today; His people preach His Gospel. The prophetic Word reveals that a horrible judgment will come upon this world. The only escape that God has provided is through faith in Jesus Christ. There is still time to belong to the group the Apostle Paul described in his letter to the Thessalonians: "to wait for his Son from heaven, whom he raised from the dead, even Jesus, which delivered us from the wrath to come" (1 Thessalonians 1:10).

The only escape that God has provided is through faith in Jesus Christ.

Destructive judgment will come upon the world, but there is a way out: "For God hath not appointed us to wrath, but to obtain salvation by our Lord Jesus Christ" (1 Thessalonians 5:9).

Chapter 5 paints a prophetic picture of the Gentile world. In spite of the offer of grace, forgiveness and restoration, the Gentiles defy the living God and will continue to do so until their ultimate demise. When God finally sends the judgment that leads to condemnation against the nations of the world, we read: "And the kings of the earth, and the great men, and the rich men, and the chief captains, and the mighty men, and every bondman, and every free man, hid themselves in the dens and in the rocks of the mountains; and said to the mountains and rocks, Fall on us, and hide us from the face of him that sitteth on the throne, and from the wrath of the Lamb" (Revelation 6:15–16). Instead of repenting, the people will try to hide behind God's creation. They will expect the rocks and mountains to save them, but they will refuse to humble themselves under the mighty hand of the Creator.

Chapter **6**

DANIEL IN THE LION'S DEN

"It pleased Darius to set over the kingdom an hundred and twenty princes, which should be over the whole kingdom; And over these three presidents; of whom Daniel was first: that the princes might give accounts unto them, and the king should have no damage. Then this Daniel was preferred above the presidents and princes, because an excellent spirit was in him; and the king thought to set him over the whole realm" (Daniel 6:1–3).

One of the most exciting stories in the Bible is that of Daniel in the lion's den, an account that documents how Daniel trusted in God without any reservations. His character serves as a unique portrayal of Jesus Christ, the Righteous One who was to come.

Daniel's status had already been elevated under the rule of King Nebuchadnezzar. "Then the king made Daniel a great man, and gave him many great gifts, and made him ruler over the whole province of Babylon, and chief of the governors over all the wise men of Babylon" (Daniel 2:48).

Daniel remained in power after the Media-Persian Empire defeated Babylon, the first Gentile super-power. This is unusual because the leaders of a defeated nation were usually executed; however, Daniel was above matters of nationality. He served the living God, the God of Israel who created heaven and earth, and with whom there are no national boundaries or obstacles because He is supreme.

Darius, king of the second Gentile superpower, recognized Daniel's value and elevated him to the highest position: "over these three presidents; of whom Daniel was first" (Daniel 6:2).

Conspiracy unto Death

Daniel served the king without any hidden agenda. His perfect walk before the king — and more importantly before God — gave occasion to his fellow presidents to become the subject of jealousy. Even more, it invited them to plot a conspiracy for his death.

"Then the presidents and princes sought to find occasion against Daniel concerning the kingdom; but they could find none occasion nor fault; forasmuch as he was faithful, neither was there any error or fault found in him" (verse 4). Jealousy was to be expected because Daniel was a foreigner, a Jew, a defeated enemy who was brought to Babylon. Yet this new-comer was placed above all the presidents and princes. That didn't go over well with the locals. But Daniel was faithful to the king and to his God; they could not find any fault in him. He already followed in the footsteps of the One who was to come.

> "For he hath made him to be sin for us, who knew no sin; that we might be made the righteousness of God in him."

Later in history, Jesus challenged the religious authority in Jerusalem: "Which of you convinceth me of sin?" (John 8:46). In 2 Corinthians 5:21, Paul testified: "For he hath made him to be sin for us, who knew no sin; that we might be made the righteousness of God in him."

The Irreversible Law

Daniel's enemies reveal a unique characteristic of this Gentile superstructure: "Now, O king, establish the decree, and sign the writing, that it be not changed, according to the law of the Medes and

Persians, which altereth not. Wherefore king Darius signed the writing and the decree" (Daniel 6:8–9). The law was irreversible. This reminds us of Scripture's statement: "The soul that sinneth, it shall die" (Ezekiel 18:4).

Daniel must have had a strong testimony in the presence of the people. They knew he trusted in the God of Israel and were aware of his faithful and persistent prayer life. Apparently, they knew Daniel had a stronger faith in God than in any man-made law. This was a clever, premeditated conspiracy that would guarantee Daniel's end once and for all.

After the king had signed the new law that was effective for 30 days, we read: "Now when Daniel knew that the writing was signed, he went into his house; and his windows being open in his chamber toward Jerusalem, he kneeled upon his knees three times a day, and prayed, and gave thanks before his God, as he did aforetime" (verse 10).

It seems strange that Daniel honored God instead of pleading with Him. Scripture says he gave thanks.

Furthermore, he made no efforts to hide his prayer life because of the enemies: "Then these men assembled, and found Daniel praying and making supplication before his God" (verse 11). Daniel ignored the political reality. He lived in the presence of God, trusted Him, served Him and followed Him.

Daniel hadn't changed; he wasn't influenced and didn't compromise. His trademark characteristic was that he "purposed in his heart that he would not defile himself with the portion of the king's meat" (Daniel 1:8).

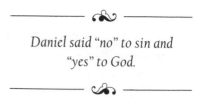

Daniel said "no" to sin and "yes" to God.

Daniel said "no" to sin and "yes" to God. He lived his life on the foundation of that truth and served the living God in spirit and the political authority in the flesh.

The Case Against the Law

Daniel didn't go into hiding. Because of his true character, he had nothing to fear: "Then these men assembled, and found Daniel praying and making supplication before his God. Then they came near, and spake before the king concerning the king's decree; Hast thou not signed a decree, that every man that shall ask a petition of any God or man within thirty days, save of thee, O king, shall be cast into the den of lions? The king answered and said, The thing is true, according to the law of the Medes and Persians, which altereth not. Then answered they and said before the king, That Daniel, which is of the children of the captivity of Judah, regardeth not thee, O king, nor the decree that thou hast signed, but maketh his petition three times a day" (verses 11–13).

Daniel's enemies tried to silence the prophet and the truth of God.

Daniel's enemies were enemies of the prophetic

Word. They tried to silence the prophet and consequently the truth of God. They found Daniel praying and heard his prayer. As witnesses, according to the law they could appear before the king and accuse Daniel of being a lawbreaker.

Now Daniel was condemned to die, not for his own sins but because of the sins of others. Here again we see a picture of Jesus, the sinless One who died for the sins of others. The Lord loved us while we were yet sinners.

The King Who Could Not Save

King Darius was overwhelmed with compassion for Daniel: "Then the king, when he heard these words, was sore displeased with himself, and set his heart on Daniel to deliver him: and he laboured till the going down of the sun to deliver him" (Daniel 6:14). But even the king could not deliver Daniel. The law was in place and could not be changed: "Know, O king, that the law of the Medes and Persians is, that no decree nor statute which the king establisheth may be changed" (verse 15).

It is important to note how much King Darius loved and respected Daniel, and even trusted in the God of Israel: "Now the king spake and said unto Daniel, thy God whom thou servest continually, he will deliver thee" (verse 16).

Time for Execution

From the enemies' perspective, the execution was a done deal. "They brought Daniel, and cast him into the den of lions...And a stone was brought, and laid upon the mouth of the den; and the king sealed it with his own signet, and with the signet of his lords; that the purpose might not be changed concerning Daniel" (Daniel 6:16a–17).

Long before Daniel was born another faithful servant of the Lord named David, who identified with Jesus, the Suffering Servant, had exclaimed: "My God, my God, why hast thou forsaken me?" (Psalm 22:1). He described his enemies as roaring lions (verse 13) and prophetically depicted the crucifixion: "they pierced my hands and my feet" (verse 16). In verse 21, David had exclaimed: "Save me from the lion's mouth." David was unjustly persecuted; thus, he was able to utter these words. He prophetically participated in the suffering of Jesus. Later, the Apostle Peter wrote: "But rejoice, inasmuch as ye are partakers of Christ's sufferings; that, when his glory shall be revealed, ye may be glad also with exceeding joy" (1 Peter 4:13).

Silence

King Darius represents a prophetic picture of our heavenly Father, who was silent when His Son suffered. The Father did not answer when Jesus cried, "My God, my God, why hast thou forsaken me?" Likewise, Darius departed from the place of Daniel's execution. Verse 18 says: "Then the king went to his palace, and passed the night fasting: neither were instruments of musick brought before him: and his sleep went from him."

Although Scripture doesn't offer us details, we can imagine that Daniel's enemies must have celebrated their victory and rejoiced over the success of their plan to destroy the enemy. But they celebrated too soon.

The Act of Grace

"Then the king arose very early in the morning, and went in haste unto the den of lions. And when he came to the den, he cried with a lamentable voice unto Daniel: and the king spake and said to Daniel, O Daniel, servant of the living God, is thy God, whom thou servest continually, able to deliver thee from the lions?" (verses 19–20). This pagan king expressed his compassionate desire for Daniel's well being: "He cried with a lamentable voice." Then came the answer of victory: "O king, live for ever. My God hath sent his angel, and hath shut the lions' mouths, that they have not hurt me: forasmuch as before him innocency was found in me; and also before thee, O king, have I done no hurt. Then was the king exceeding glad for him, and commanded that they should take Daniel up out of the den. So Daniel was taken up out of the den, and no manner of hurt was found upon him, because he believed in his God" (verses 21–23).

Salvation Is of the Jews

Here is another prophetic picture of the Jewish people. They are different; they are foreigners, outsiders who have been rejected by the world. But from these Jews came Jesus Christ, the Savior who testified that salvation is of the Jews. The world will turn against the Jewish people, against Jerusalem, and thereby against the Lord and His Anointed during the Great Tribulation. They may think that their victory is a sure thing, but the prophetic Word clearly describes that the salvation of Israel will be the destruction of the enemies.

Such was the case when the Jews were slaves in Egypt. When judgment came, it led to Israel's salvation and Egypt's destruction. So it will be in the end.

Jeremiah, a contemporary of Daniel, wrote: "Alas! for that day is great, so that none is like it: it is even the time of Jacob's trouble; but he shall be saved out of it" (Jeremiah 30:7).

The key to Daniel's victory was his faith in the living God. Likewise, faith in the finished work of Jesus Christ on Calvary's cross is the key to our salvation today.

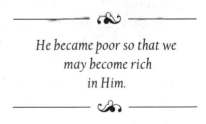

He became poor so that we may become rich in Him.

The birth of Christ is traditionally known as "Christmas," the time when we remember His incarnation. His birth was unannounced, He was virtually unknown, and He arrived in poverty. He became poor so that we may become rich in Him. Jesus came to serve and to die for mankind, but He arose victoriously on the third day. The Gospel of salvation continues to be proclaimed until this day.

The New Law

For King Darius and Daniel, the law could not be reversed; therefore, a new law had to be issued. Daniel's enemies came under the jurisdiction of this new law: "And the king commanded, and they brought those men which had accused Daniel, and they cast them into the den of lions, them, their children, and their wives; and the lions had the mastery of them, and brake all their bones in pieces or ever they came at the bottom of the den" (verse 24).

Here we are reminded of the new law put into effect through the shedding of Jesus' blood on Calvary's cross. The old law, however, has not been invalidated: "The soul that sinneth, it shall die" (Ezekiel 18:4). But there is a new law: "A new commandment I give unto you, That ye love one another; as I have loved you, that ye also love one another" (John 13:34). This law supercedes all others and is infinitely greater than the entire collection of laws given to Israel. This is a serious warning for all Christians who attempt to please God by keeping some type of law, whether it is biblical or not. Scripture says: "Cursed is every one that continueth not in all things which are written in the book of the law to do them" (Galatians 3:10).

Darius the Missionary

King Darius became a voice for the God of Israel: "Then king Darius wrote unto all people, nations, and languages, that dwell in all the earth; Peace be multiplied unto you. I make a decree, that in every dominion of my kingdom men tremble and fear before the God of Daniel: for he is the living God, and stedfast for ever, and his kingdom that which shall not be destroyed, and his dominion shall be even unto the end. He delivereth and rescueth, and he worketh signs and wonders in heaven and in earth, who hath delivered Daniel from the power of the lions" (Daniel 6:25–27).

Summary

Chapter 6 concludes God's testimony through Daniel the Jew against the god of this world. God exposed the political powers and its religions through these faithful Jewish servants. The first of the six chapters speak of the origin of Daniel and his three friends. Chapter 2 prophetically shows what will happen to the entire world; the Gentile nations will be destroyed by an act of God: "the stone that smote the image became the great mountain and filled the whole earth."

Next we read about Shadrach, Meshach and Abednego in the fiery furnace. Nebuchadnezzar's attempt to create a global religion failed. Instead of being burned to death these three men were elevated: "Then the king promoted Shadrach, Meshach, and

Abednego, in the province of Babylon" (Daniel 3:30).

Chapter 4 records the testimony of King Nebuchadnezzar, identified as the "gold" ruler of the Gentile nations. He confessed, repented and recognized the God of Israel.

In Chapter 5 we see King Belshazzar represent the end of the Babylonian kingdom and prophetically show the inability to repent during the endtimes. Just as Belshazzar did not repent when he heard the thunderous voice of judgment when Daniel interpreted the handwriting on the wall, so, too, will the people refuse to repent when God sends judgment upon the world: "And men were scorched with great heat, and blasphemed the name of God, which hath power over these plagues: and they repented not to give him glory" (Revelation 16:9).

The first six chapters of the book of Daniel reveal history on the earth; the next six chapters reveal the earth's future from a heavenly perspective.

Chapter 7

THE FIRST VISION OF THE INVISIBLE WORLD

"In the first year of Belshazzar king of Babylon Daniel had a dream and visions of his head upon his bed: then he wrote the dream, and told the sum of the matters. Daniel spake and said, I saw in my vision by night, and, behold, the four winds of the heaven strove upon the great sea" (Daniel 7:1–2).

Chapter 6 ended with these words: "So this Daniel prospered in the reign of Darius, and in the reign of Cyrus the Persian" (Daniel 6:28). Daniel served a foreign king in a foreign country and spoke a foreign language, yet he served his God and his new country even though they were enemies respon-

Daniel served His God and his new country even though they were enemies responsible for the destruction of his own nation, the city of Jerusalem and the temple on Mount Moriah.

sible for the destruction of his own nation, the city of Jerusalem, and the temple on Mount Moriah.

The Invisible World

Now we turn our attention from the visible to the invisible. When Daniel wrote, "the four winds of heaven," he was referring to the entire Gentile history from Babylon to Mystery Babylon. He was reporting the mighty movement taking place in the invisible world. The German Menge translation puts it this way: "And I saw how the four winds of the heavens with mighty commotions disturbed the great sea." This reminds us of Revelation 13:1: "And I stood upon the sand of the sea, and saw a beast rise up out of the sea, having seven heads and ten horns, and upon his horns ten crowns, and upon his heads the name of blasphemy." Revelation 17:15 explains what that sea is: "The waters which thou sawest, where the whore sitteth, are peoples, and multitudes, and nations, and tongues." Thus, we are entering the darkness of the world of wickedness that Paul wrote about: "For we wrestle not against flesh and blood, but against principalities, against powers, against the rulers of the darkness of this world, against spiritual wickedness in high places" (Ephesians 6:12).

Let's take a closer look at this Scripture that foretells the future: "And four great beasts came up from the sea, diverse one from another. The first was like a lion, and had eagle's wings: I beheld till the wings thereof were plucked, and it was lifted up from the earth, and made stand upon the feet as a man, and a man's heart was given to it. And behold another beast, a second, like to a bear, and it raised up itself on one side, and it had three ribs in the mouth of it between the teeth of it: and they said thus unto it, Arise, devour much flesh. After this I beheld, and lo another, like a leopard, which had upon the back of it four wings of a fowl; the beast had also four heads; and dominion was given to it" (Daniel 7:3–6).

This again is a summary vision from a heavenly perspective showing the entire Gentile world, depicted by the four great beasts. When we consider Scripture in its proper simplicity, we begin to understand that Daniel's prophecies are indeed made easy. Of course countless books have been written about other great nations, empires and kingdoms, but none of these entities plays an integral role in the events that transpire in the Gentile world. We do not go wrong when we follow this simple pattern: Babylon,

Media-Persia, Greece, Rome. Rome is listed last because the Bible says a new kingdom will be established in the days of these kings, a kingdom that will destroy the previous ones and will be eternal.

The Beasts Leading the Nations

Here we see the nations represented by demonic powers symbolized by animals. This is the work of another figure that is also compared with an animal: "And the great dragon was cast out, that old serpent, called the Devil, and Satan, which deceiveth the whole world: he was cast out into the earth, and his angels were cast out with him" (Revelation 12:9). Generally, an animal is also called a beast. We all know that the distinction between man and animal is grounded in God's declaration: "Let us make man in our image" (Genesis 1:26). Therefore, it is not surprising that rebellious man expresses his desire to behave like an animal in these endtimes.

Even today, animals are used as symbols for the nations. For example, the eagle is the national symbol of Germany, Austria and a number of other European countries, including the United States. The bear usually represents Russia and the dragon, China. The lion is the symbol of Ethiopia, the UK and several other nations.

However, these animal symbols do not directly apply to the prophetic Word. It is futile to try to identify today's nations by their animal symbols.

Doubtless it has secondary significance, but it's not the real thing.

I believe these animal symbols are directly related to the demonic powers, which are subject to the "great dragon...that old serpent, called the Devil, and Satan."

While chapter 2 contains a simple overview of the Gentile nations in the image of a man, chapter 7 reveals the spiritual substance and provides more details, especially from a heavenly perspective.

The Babylonian kingdom, represented by a lion, comes first; the Media-Persian kingdom, pictured as a bear, is next; the Grecian empire, depicted as a leopard, is third; and the final one is separated from the other three. Verse 7 says: "After this I saw in the night visions, and behold a fourth beast, dreadful and terrible, and strong exceedingly; and it had great iron teeth: it devoured and brake in pieces, and stamped the residue with the feet of it: and it was diverse from all the beasts that were before it; and it had ten horns." When we deal with the fourth beast, we are advised to take special notice, particularly of the word "diverse."

How "Diverse" is the Fourth Beast?

The words used to describe the fourth beast are: "dreadful," "terrible," and "strong exceedingly."

This is a negative description of the fourth and final Gentile world empire because no such things were said about the first three beasts. They all became strong, conquered and subdued other nations, and generated riches and power in order to solidify their rule.

Conquer and Divide

That's how it's always been. In fact, the sword was used to establish Israel. Jericho was the first city the Jews conquered after crossing the Jordan River when they entered the Promised Land: "And they utterly destroyed all that was in the city, both man and woman, young and old, and ox, and sheep, and ass, with the edge of the sword" (Joshua 6:21). That was God's judgment upon a heathen nation.

We must point out that Israel's conquest of Canaan was different from the wars of all other nations because it was ordered by God Himself. He commanded the Israelites to show no mercy and destroy everything in order to show that sin will not be tolerated and must be paid for. God used Israel because it was chosen to be His tool of judgment. The Israelites were not blameless themselves; God judged them in turn through the Gentile nations, as was the case during Daniel's time.

The conquer-and-divide principle has been practiced until today, although with a distinct difference: Israel was commanded to destroy every living thing, including valuable livestock. Most wars fought since then have been waged to gain livestock, people and material. Wars always have winners and losers.

A New Area

Ironically, the conquer-and-divide philosophy ended in 1948 when Israel became a nation. All the nations forbade Israel to take possession of the Promised Land territory it had conquered. In fact, the United States unequivocally ordered Israel to withdraw from territory it won in 1956, 1967 and 1973. This isn't often mentioned, but is important because a change is taking place for the first time in Gentile history.

The Fourth Beast

What's so different about this fourth beast? We've already learned that it was dreadful, terrible and exceedingly strong, so let's go one step further to ask what it does. First, it devours; second, it breaks into pieces; and third, it stamps to residue with its feet.

To "devour" means to take possession of what has been conquered. To "break into pieces" means to annihilate the conquered nation's laws, traditions and cultures. To "stamp to residue with its feet" means to establish total dominion over the conquered ones.

For example, the Indians, the original inhabitants of what is now the United States, were "devoured," "broken" and "stamped" into submission. It is safe to say that the chances of reversing their defeat are slim to none.

The entire world is living during the period of the fourth beast, but that beast, as we learned in chapter 2, is part of the one image. That means the entire

Gentile world, from Babylon to Mystery Babylon.

Of course, our society has developed to a rather sophisticated level. In most cases, liberty and justice have been granted to the majority of the people. We no longer conquer lands for the sake of expanding our own boundaries; that's history. From an earthly perspective, we can claim to be a peaceful society. We have a high standard of living, a great quality of life, and respect for other cultures, societies and nations. But although we seem to be relatively good people in our own eyes, a heavenly perspective offers a completely different story. Our democratic civilization falls into the categories of "dreadful," "terrible," "strong exceedingly" and "it devours...it breaks to pieces...and stamps the residue with its feet."

One Nation Under God?

I am fully aware this is a difficult concept for nationalists to grasp because they have been deceived into believing their nation is more godly, righteous and peaceful than all others. But that is the spirit of Antichrist, who exalts himself above all that is of God. Therefore, if believers say their nation is special and that they have been blessed by God, they are following in the spirit of the father of lies. About him, Isaiah wrote: "For thou hast said in thine heart, I will ascend into heaven, I will exalt my throne above the stars of God: I will sit also upon the mount of the congregation, in the sides of the north" (Isaiah 14:13).

History Documents Brutality

History documents wars, bloodshed and cruelty among the so-called "Western" nations, particularly Europe. But we don't have to look any farther than at our own country, where hardship, danger, poverty and death have always been the order of the day.

For example, not too long ago, African-Americans weren't even considered human beings and could be sold as slaves on the open market. The overwhelming majority of European immigrants were indigent servants who barely made a living. Then came the Civil War, which showed the ugly truth of how brother can turn against brother. Pain, suffering and hardship were the results.

Of course, we like to indulge in our own propaganda that says we are a peaceful nation founded on biblical principles. Lovely as that sounds, it has no relationship to either earthly or heavenly perspectives.

The False Peace

The fourth beast empire of our time is in the process of producing a counterfeit 1,000-year kingdom of peace! A clue to that development is contained in the last five words of Daniel 7:7: "and it had ten horns." Horns symbolize power, and power comes from God — but there is a substitute.

Power of Materialism

The god of materialism is worshipped around the globe. Even during the Great Tribulation, when God's destructive judgment will be unleashed, "the rest of the men which were not killed by these plagues yet repented not of the works of their hands, that they should not worship devils, and idols of gold, and silver, and brass, and stone, and of wood: which neither can see, nor hear, nor walk" (Revelation 9:20). These men will not repent "of their murders, nor of their sorceries, nor of their fornication, nor of their thefts."

_____ ❧ _____

"For then shall be great tribulation, such as was not since the beginning of the world to this time, no, nor ever shall be."

_____ ❧ _____

The world is being taken captive by the system of the fourth beast, which is diverse from any other system. This system we call "freedom" and "democracy" will usher in the time Jesus referred to in Matthew 24:21: "For then shall be great tribulation, such as was not since the beginning of the world to this time, no, nor ever shall be."

When Negative Is Considered Positive

Which negative behaviors are being accepted by virtually the entire world, particularly the West? "This know also, that in the last days perilous times shall come. For men shall be:

1. lovers of their own selves
2. covetous
3. boasters
4. proud

120

5. blasphemers
6. disobedient to parents
7. unthankful
8. unholy
9. without natural affection
10. trucebreakers
11. false accusers
12. incontinent
13. fierce
14. despisers of those that are good
15. traitors
16. heady
17. highminded
18. lovers of pleasures more than lovers of God" (2 Timothy 3:1–4).

The late Dr. Wim Malgo, founder of Midnight Call Ministries, used to preach on this passage of Scripture. As he identified these 18 characteristics that will characterize the generation of the end-times, he pointed out that the number 18 is made up of three sixes. These types of behaviors are becoming prevalent in today's society.

Today, religion is considered en vogue, self-confidence is at an all-time high, and self-esteem not only is promoted in the world but in many churches around the world.

Verse 5 describes our current day: "Having a form of godliness, but denying the power thereof:

from such turn away" (verse 5). Today, religion is considered en vogue, self-confidence is at an all-time high, and self-esteem not only is promoted in the world but in many churches around the world. Take a trip to your local Christian bookstore and read some of the titles that line the shelves. The majority of the books are aimed at self-help and cover topics such as: how to have a better marriage, how to be a better husband or wife, and how to raise better children. It's all about the betterment of self; rather than "more about Jesus," it is "more about me." That is the trademark of the final world empire that was, and is, and is to come.

We mustn't assume this will develop sometime in the future. The same enemy present when Jesus was crucified is the same one who imitates Jesus and offers a substitute to the Church today. Things will become more visible in the end stages of the endtimes.

Recently I heard a report on our local BBN station regarding self-esteem:

Studies Link Violence with Self-Love

'For men shall be lovers of their own selves, covetous, boasters, proud, blasphemers, disobedient to parents, unthankful, unholy' (2 Timothy 3:2).

Popular psychology has for years declared that troubled young people, especially those who become violent, suffer from low self-esteem. But three studies released in the summer of 1999 conclude the opposite: young people who become violent have too much self-esteem.

One of the studies published by the American Psychological Association observed 540 undergraduate students. After answering standard questions designed to measure self-esteem and narcissism, the students were put into different situations. They were given the opportunity to act aggressively against someone who had praised them, insulted them or did nothing to them. Researchers found that the most narcissistic students were the most likely to react violently. They also found that narcissists were especially aggressive against anyone who had offended them. Another study found narcissism is prevalent among prisoners convicted of rape, murder, assault, armed robbery and similar crimes. When their self-esteem was measured against the general population, it was found to be above average. The researchers involved In this study pointed out that the primary focus of prison rehabilitation is on building self-esteem. This, they concluded, is definitely the wrong approach, sInce such people already have an inflated view of themselves.

The Bible warns against narcissism. Many of the problems in our society today are undoubtedly the result of this condition. (*Toronto Star*, 12/99 p.J6 "Studies link violence and narcissism").

The "Breaking" Continues

Murder of the unborn is a legal act, and in most

cases is even paid for by the government. Homosexuals demand special rights and benefits. They fight to be recognized as married couples. Doesn't this remind us of what Jesus said about the times being like Sodom and Gomorrah when He returns?

But let's not condemn those who are involved with such atrocities as abortion and unnatural unions. Let's look at ourselves: What's happened to the Christian marriage? Do we take our wedding vows seriously? Apparently not, because more Christian marriages end in divorce than marriages among unbelievers. The United States leads the world in this respect.

Having said this, we can summarize that the times are getting better in a material sense, but spiritually, they are marked by the threefold criteria: 1) it devours; 2) it breaks to pieces; 3) it stamps the residue with its feet.

Ten Horns

We already mentioned that power is represented by horns. The fourth beast, the last Gentile superpower, had ten horns. The number 10 stands for fullness or completion. God gave Moses the Ten Commandments. He sent ten plagues upon Egypt. Abraham prayed for ten righteous people within the wicked city of Sodom. The ten horns represent the tenfold power structure of the last empire on planet Earth.

But there is more: "I considered the horns, and, behold, there came up among them another little horn, before whom there were three of the first horns plucked up by the roots: and, behold, in this horn were eyes like the eyes of man, and a mouth speaking great things" (verse 8). Now God shows us there will be a conflict within that conflict during this endtime power structure. The key figure of the final Gentile world will arise with "a mouth speaking great things."

Again, we must point out that the fourth beast, the ten horns and everything connected with this vision belongs to the whole world. For example, it is wrong to try and identify ten nations in Europe or, as we often hear and read, the reestablishment of the Roman Empire. From a biblical perspective, this is incorrect because the Roman Empire never ceased to exist. Even in chapter 2, we see that the whole world will be concerned when Jesus destroys the Gentile power structure. "Then was the iron, the clay, the brass, the silver, and the gold, broken to pieces together, and became like the chaff of the summer threshingfloors; and the wind carried them away, that no place was found for them: and the stone that smote the image became a great mountain, and filled the whole earth" (Daniel 2:35).

In his explanation to King Nebuchadnezzar, Daniel spoke of the silver and brass kingdom, "which shall bear rule over all the earth." In Nebuchadnezzar's testimony recorded in chapter 4, Daniel said, " And thy dominion to the end of the earth." This is true globalism. From God's perspective, there is only one world: that of the Gentiles. In this world, there is only one Israel and that's the small country east of the Mediterranean. "A mouth speaking great things" doesn't refer to only one person, but represents the entire world — all 200-plus nations on all five continents.

Vision of God

Daniel didn't go into any further details at that moment, but he received a heavenly vision that apparently had been meant to strengthen him: "I beheld till the thrones were cast down, and the Ancient of days did sit, whose garment was white as snow, and the hair of his head like the pure wool: his throne was like the fiery flame, and his wheels as burning fire. A fiery stream issued and came forth from before him: thousand thousands ministered unto him, and ten thousand times ten thousand stood before him: the judgment was set, and the books were opened" (verses 9–10). This was an intermission so Daniel could be assured that God will keep the victory.

The End of Evil

What will be the end of the Antichrist and his associates? "I beheld then because of the voice of the great words which the horn spake: I beheld even till the beast was slain, and his body destroyed, and given to the burning flame. As concerning the rest of the beasts, they had their dominion taken away: yet their lives were prolonged for a season and time" (verses 11–12). Daniel must have been encouraged to see the end of the fourth beast and its offspring. The book of Revelation records the end of the Antichrist and the false prophet as it says they will be "cast alive into a lake of fire burning with brimstone" (Revelation 19:20b).

The Lord's Dominion

In contrast to the fourth empire, again we see the victory of the heavenly one: "I saw in the night visions, and, behold, one like the Son of man came with the clouds of heaven, and came to the Ancient of days, and they brought him near before him. And there was given him dominion, and glory, and a kingdom, that all people, nations, and languages, should serve him: his dominion is an everlasting dominion, which shall not pass away, and his kingdom that which shall not be destroyed" (verses 13–14). Doesn't this remind us of Revelation 5:13? "And every creature which is in heaven, and on the earth, and under

"And every creature which is in heaven, and on the earth, and under the earth, and such as are in the sea, and all that are in them, heard I saying, Blessing, and honour, and glory, and power, be unto him that sitteth upon the throne, and unto the Lamb for ever and ever."

the earth, and such as are in the sea, and all that are in them, heard I saying, Blessing, and honour, and glory, and power, be unto him that sitteth upon the throne, and unto the Lamb for ever and ever."

Heavenly Explanation

Daniel saw and heard but he did not understand; however, he did the right thing. He "asked him the truth of all this. So he told me, and made me know the interpretation of the things" (verse 16). Next we read the explanation: "These great beasts, which are four, are four kings, which shall arise out of the earth. But the saints of the most High shall take the kingdom, and possess the kingdom for ever, even for ever and ever" (verses 17–18). This simple explanation contains the assurance that the Lord God and His kingdom will exist eternally.

Daniel still wasn't quite satisfied. He continued: "Then I would know the truth of the fourth beast, which was diverse from all the others, exceeding dreadful, whose teeth were of iron, and his nails of brass; which devoured, brake in pieces, and stamped the residue with his feet; And of the ten horns that were in his head, and of the other which came up, and before whom three fell; even of that horn that had eyes, and a mouth that spake very great things, whose look was more stout than his fellows. I beheld, and the same horn made war with the saints, and prevailed against them" (verses 19–21). Again, we notice that the fourth beast is different from the others. This means the entire world society will be different from all previous ones, which were limited to a relatively small geographical territory that we call the Middle East. But the fourth world empire encompasses virtually all of Europe and Europe encompasses the entire world. From that power structure will come the evil one, whom we call the Antichrist.

War Against the Saints

The Antichrist's uniqueness lies in the fact that he makes "war with the saints and prevails against them." The same could not be said of Babylon's King Nebuchadnezzar or Persia's King Darius. Blatant opposition against God has been reserved for the fourth beast and his kingdom.

Once again, Daniel received the assurance that God is in control: "Until the Ancient of days came, and judgment was given to the saints of the most High; and the time came that the saints possessed the kingdom" (verse 22).

The fourth beast is mentioned again in verses 23–25: "Thus he said, The fourth beast shall be the fourth kingdom upon earth, which shall be diverse from all kingdoms, and shall devour the whole earth, and shall tread it down, and break it in pieces. And the ten horns out of this kingdom are ten kings that shall arise: and another shall rise after them; and he shall be diverse from the first, and he shall subdue three kings. And he shall speak great words against the most High, and shall wear out the saints of the most High, and think to change times and laws: and they shall be given into his hand until a time and times and the dividing of time." It's encouraging to read that the evil one has only a limited time, in this case, 3 ¹/₂ years.

Who Are the Saints?

I would venture to say that the saints are God's chosen people, Israel, because the Church will then be in the presence of the Lord forever. Someone may object and say that Israel is a sinful nation and the Jews reject Christ as the Messiah. That is true of course, but that is their condition; it doesn't change their position. Deuteronomy 14:2 explains their position according to God's plan of salvation: "For thou art an holy people unto the LORD thy God, and the LORD hath chosen thee to be a peculiar people unto himself, above all the nations that are upon the earth." Notice the words: "The Lord hath chosen thee." That is an unconditional guarantee that depends not on circumstances, behavior or sin. Please remember that "while we were yet sinners, Christ died for us" (Romans 5:8). Scripture says we were chosen in Him before the foundation of the world (Ephesians 1:4). God is not bound to our time or to our feeble minds in regard to analyzing spiritual and eternal things.

Consider Ephesians 2:5–6: "Even when we were dead in sins, hath quickened us together with Christ, (by grace ye are saved;) And hath raised us up together, and made us sit together in heavenly places in Christ Jesus." This is a spiritual reality. This is the same God who made the statement we just read in Deuteronomy 14:2 regarding His people, Israel.

Tribulation Saints

Of course, the saints also include those who will come to believe in the Lord Jesus Christ during the Great Tribulation. Revelation 7:9 refers to them: "After this I beheld, and, lo, a great multitude, which no man could number, of all nations, and kindreds, and people, and tongues, stood before the throne, and before the Lamb, clothed with white robes, and palms in their hands." We mustn't forget that in the same chapter are listed 144,000 saints — 12,000 from each of the tribes of Israel. They are sealed, untouchable to the evil one.

Israel is first among the saints. It stands opposed to all the nations. We've already studied the first six chapters of Daniel and noticed the contrast between the nations and Daniel, his three friends and their God.

While judgment is proclaimed upon each Gentile power structure, we read this about Israel: "And in the days of these kings shall the God of heaven set up a kingdom, which shall never be destroyed: and the kingdom shall not be left to other people, but it shall break in pieces and consume all these kingdoms, and it shall stand for ever" (Daniel 2:44).

Ten Kings or Ten Nations?

We need to exercise caution when interpreting Bible prophecy because we are dealing with a heavenly vision. None of the kings or kingdoms is mentioned by name, nor is there given a geographical location; thus, we can assume this refers to the kingdom of Satan. This is activity in the demonic world.

It was assumed during the early years of the European Common Market that when this community had grown to include ten nations it would represent the ten horns and the ten kings as listed in the books of Daniel and Revelation. But that is obviously not the case. In the meantime, the European Common Market has become the "European Union" and is made up of 25 nations, with a dozen or so more standing in line with their applications for entry in hand.

In the 1960s, Dr. Wim Malgo warned, "Let us not look for ten countries as being members of the European Common Market, constituting the fulfillment of Daniel 7 and Revelation 17. Rather, we must look for ten power structures that will develop through the European initiative, but will be worldwide."

Another Comfort

Once again Daniel was comforted after seeing these developments in a vision from a heavenly perspective: "But the judgment shall sit, and they shall take away his dominion, to consume and to destroy it unto the end. And the kingdom and dominion, and the greatness of the kingdom under the whole heaven, shall be given to the people of the saints of the most High, whose kingdom is an everlasting kingdom, and all dominions shall serve and obey him" (verses 26–27).

What an encouraging chapter this is for believers! We serve the God of creation, the God of Israel who manifested Himself in the flesh when He was born of a virgin in the town of Bethlehem, in the land of Israel. He was born to die in order to pay the ransom for the sins of all people from all time. Everyone who recognizes his or her lost condition becomes an instant candidate for forgiveness by simply accepting this gift of eternal life from the hands of Jesus Christ!

Chapter 8

THE THIRD GENTILE SUPERPOWER

"In the third year of the reign of king Belshazzar a vision appeared unto me, even unto me Daniel, after that which appeared unto me at the first. And I saw in a vision; and it came to pass, when I saw, that I was at Shushan in the palace, which is in the province of Elam; and I saw in a vision, and I was by the river of Ulai" (Daniel 8:1–2).

Daniel received the second vision two years after the first one. The vision included a name — Belshazzar; a date — the third year; and an address — the place in Shushan by the river of Ulai. Daniel was on earth but the vision came from heaven.

The vision included a name – Belshazzar; a date – the third year; and an address – the place in Shushan by the river of Ulai.

"Then I lifted up mine eyes, and saw, and, behold, there stood before the river a ram which had two horns: and the two horns were high; but one was higher than the other, and the higher came up last. I saw the ram pushing westward, and northward, and southward; so that no beasts might stand before him, neither was there any that could deliver out of his hand; but he did according to his will, and became great. And as I was considering, behold, an he goat came from the west on the face of the whole earth, and touched not the ground: and the goat had a notable horn between his eyes. And he came to the ram that had two horns, which I had seen standing before the river, and ran unto him in the fury of his power. And I saw him come close unto the ram, and he was moved with choler against him, and smote the ram, and brake his two horns: and there was no power in the ram to stand before him, but he cast him down to the ground, and stamped upon him: and there was none

136

that could deliver the ram out of his hand. Therefore the he goat waxed very great: and when he was strong, the great horn was broken; and for it came up four notable ones toward the four winds of heaven. And out of one of them came forth a little horn, which waxed exceeding great, toward the south, and toward the east, and toward the pleasant land" (verses 3–9).

Clues such as the phrases, "on the face of the whole earth" and "towards the four winds of heaven" lead us to conclude that this vision unveiled the entire history of the Gentile world. Again, these visions are from a heavenly perspective, in contrast to the first six chapters of the book of Daniel, which contain an earthly report that includes clear descriptions, times and locations. But from a heavenly perspective, the past, present and future are all one. With God a thousand years is as one day and one day is as a thousand years. He is the same yesterday, today and forever.

Daniel saw the future. This vision was twofold: 1) It described what would happen to Daniel's people and 2) It outlined what will happen to the world.

The Ram and the Goat

Verses 20 and 21 describe the identities of the ram and the goat: "The ram which thou sawest having two horns are the kings of Media and Persia. And the rough goat is the king of Grecia: and the great horn that is between his eyes is the first king." Media and

Persia, the twin power structure referred to by the phrase "two horns," would follow Babylon. The king of Greece would replace them, but "the great horn [would be] broken." That sets the stage for a new power structure, the final one through which Satan will literally rule the world.

The kingdoms of Media-Persia and Greece are indicated to be "on the face of the whole earth" (verse 5). It doesn't matter whether the Grecian Empire was limited to a small triangle between Europe, Asia and Africa; we have to take this from a heavenly perspective and that is "on the face of the whole earth."

The Beginning of Antichrist

"And out of one of them came forth a little horn, which waxed exceeding great, toward the south, and toward the east, and toward the pleasant land" (Daniel 8:9). We must take special note of verse 9 for two reasons: First, the little horn seems to belong to the Greek power structure represented by a goat. Yet there is clear indication that he overlaps into the next kingdom, the diverse one that we read about in Daniel 7:23: "the fourth kingdom upon earth, which shall be diverse from all kingdoms, and shall devour the whole earth, and shall tread it down, and break it in pieces."

Second, the power structure moves toward "the pleasant land." Surely this refers to Israel. Martin Luther translated the phrase as the "worthy land."

The next verse identifies this little horn as the devil himself: "And it waxed great, even to the host of heaven; and it cast down some of the host and of the stars to the ground, and stamped upon them" (verse 10). We read confirmation of this in Revelation 12:3–4: "And there appeared another wonder in heaven; and behold a great red dragon, having seven heads and ten horns, and seven crowns upon his heads. And his tail drew the third part of the stars of heaven, and did cast them to the earth." These verses reveal we are dealing with the power structures of the invisible world, the devil and his fallen angels, the demons.

While the goat is clearly identified as Greece, we can't assume it is limited to that power structure, which is also identified as the brass kingdom (chapter 2). They are all one; there is only one devil and he took one-third of the angelic host with him. He is God's enemy, not mankind's, because the majority of mankind follows the devil.

We must not allow ourselves to become confused by earthly developments when receiving heavenly visions described in Holy Scripture. I have not yet read a prophecy-related book that doesn't ask: "What about America?" From an earthly perspective the US is definitely a distinct political and geographic identity, but from a heavenly perspective it belongs to Satan, the king of all nations. A misunderstanding of this fact can cause great confusion and can lead us down the wrong path.

Continuing to keep in mind that this vision is from a heavenly perspective, we need to understand that the first vision in chapter 7 and the second in chapter 8 are primarily focusing on the evil one: "Yea, he magnified himself even to the prince of the host, and by him the daily sacrifice was taken away, and the place of his sanctuary was cast down. And an host was given him against the daily sacrifice by reason of transgression, and it cast down the truth to the ground; and it practised, and prospered" (verses 11–12). That is the mystery of iniquity.

A Heavenly Question

At this point, even heaven raised a question: "Then I heard one saint speaking, and another saint said unto that certain saint which spake, How long shall be the vision concerning the daily sacrifice, and the transgression of desolation, to give both the sanctuary and the host to be trodden under foot?"(verse 13). One heavenly messenger asked the other a question regarding the duration of time. Either this heavenly messenger did not know the answer or he asked the question because Daniel did not mention this apparently important issue. Thus, the other messenger replied: "And he said unto me, Unto two thousand and three hundred days; then shall the sanctuary be cleansed" (verse 14). From the words "he said unto me" we can determine that this was not a heavenly discussion between the messengers but the answer was for Daniel, who wrote it down so we would have that information.

There are many commentaries and interpretations and schools of thought about the 2,300 days mentioned here. I don't have an answer other than that this vision is from heaven. If we try to interpret this from our perspective, using our understanding of time, we are in danger of getting off track.

Daniel's Encounter with God

Next it was Daniel's turn: "And it came to pass, when I, even I Daniel, had seen the vision, and sought for the meaning, then, behold, there stood before me as the appearance of a man. And I heard a man's voice between the banks of Ulai, which called, and said, Gabriel, make this man to understand the vision. So he came near where I stood: and when he came, I was afraid, and fell upon my face: but he said unto me, Understand, O son of man: for at the time of the end shall be the vision" (verses 15–17). Gabriel didn't explain the 2,300 days, but he spoke to Daniel ("O son of man") and told him straightforwardly that "at the time of the end shall be the vision."

Daniel, obviously overwhelmed, fell into a "deep sleep." Martin Luther's translation indicates that Daniel became unconscious. This really puts such flippant remarks as "the Lord said to me" or "God told me" in their proper place. Such light-hearted, often-degrading comments are not biblical. The prophets became utterly powerless after they had an encounter with God or with one of His messengers.

The Beginning and End of Greece

At this point, Daniel needed literal, physical support; he had to be set upright. Then he said, "Behold, I will make thee know what shall be in the last end of the indignation: for at the time appointed the end shall be. The ram which thou sawest having two horns are the kings of Media and Persia. And the rough goat is the king of Grecia: and the great horn that is between his eyes is the first king. Now that being broken, whereas four stood up for it, four kingdoms shall stand up out of the nation, but not in his power" (verses 19–22). This describes the ram and goat: Media-Persia and Greece. But let's not forget that the pictures of the "ram and goat" are demonic power structures that use the nations.

In other words, Media-Persia and Greece are only a result of the activity in the demonic world. The devil and his demons rule planet Earth. They have a strategy that aims at displacing God's ultimate authority over this demon-infested world. We must add that they have a legal right to all nations because all have sinned. Therefore the demons base their claim on the verse, "He that committeth sin is of the devil" (1 John 3:8). Based on God's righteousness, there would be no hope for anyone to escape from Satan's clutches but because God is also love, "For God so loved the world," He provided an escape: "He that believeth on the Son hath everlasting life: and he that believeth not the Son shall not see life; but the wrath of God abideth on him" (John 3:36).

The Glory of Greece

Those demonic powers transfer their activity to Alexander the Great, whose kingdom was later divided into "four kingdoms" and would not be as powerful as they were under Alexander the Great. But I must emphasize that this is referring to demonic power structures; only the visible manifestation can be interpreted as being Greece.

Once again, we must remember that these visions describe a national entity from a heavenly perspective. From that perspective, Greece is a brutal nation. But from an earthly perspective, we praise the great culture we have inherited from the Greeks. Our democratic system originates with Greece. Think about all the great philosophers, inventors, and orators who came from Greece. The Greeks have every earthly reason to think they live in the greatest nation of all, but from a heavenly angle, it's just the opposite.

I hope we've learned to view our own nation in the same manner. The world lies in sin, darkness and evil. Powerful demonic princes from the underworld rule this nation. Our country is subject to Satan and his servants no matter what we think and no matter how many times we say, "God bless America." The Bible says all people are sinners, corrupt children of Satan who indulge in the pleasures of this world.

The Enemies of God's Institution

When we read the words "daily sacrifice" and "sanctuary," we can title this verse: "Satan's servants rule the world and destroy God's ordained institution."

Still missing here is the identification of the fourth and final Gentile superpower: Rome. But when we continue to read we notice that it is not necessary because Satan controls the entire world; he is the ultimate master of evil.

Daniel received the details of his success: "And an host was given him against the daily sacrifice by reason of transgression, and it cast down the truth to the ground; and it practised, and prospered" (verse 12). Three issues are mentioned:

1) The elimination of God's institution [sacrifice];
2) The casting of truth to the ground [deception will rule];
3) The prospering of man and his system [success].

Antichrist Receives Power

The Antichrist was revealed in Gabriel's explanation: "And his power shall be mighty, but not by his own power: and he shall destroy wonderfully, and shall prosper, and practise, and shall destroy the mighty and the holy people. And through his policy also he shall cause craft to prosper in his hand; and he shall magnify himself in his heart, and by peace shall destroy many: he shall also stand up against the Prince of princes; but he shall be broken without hand" (verses 24–25).

This will be the most successful man in the world. In fact, he will be a man according to the heart of man. He will become prosperous, which is exactly what the world strives to achieve.

Notice the words "but not in his power." Because he won't have any power on his own, he will receive it from Satan, as is revealed in Revelation 13:2–7. Notice the words "gave" and "given." The Antichrist will receive power from the dragon, the "old serpent, called the Devil, and Satan" (Revelation 12:9).

Antichrist's Aim is False Peace

What do the phrases "He shall destroy wonderfully" and "by peace [he] shall destroy many" mean? The Hebrew/English translation reads, "He will be extraordinarily destructive...by his cunning he will use deceit successfully." An understanding of this question is fundamental. The devil uses various means, whether demons, governments, or just regular people, to give humanity exactly what its heart desires. The Antichrist will be the product of man's desire, someone men can trust, believe, honor and even worship.

Too often we identify the evils in this world by pointing an accusing finger at someone and saying, "he's the problem." But from a scriptural perspective we know that most people are servants of Satan. As servants of the devil, however, they are creating a civilized society with a goal of challenging the fulfillment of the prophetic Word — namely, the implementation of the 1,000-year kingdom of peace. So when we read passages of Scripture such as, "He shall destroy wonderfully" and "By peace [he] shall destroy many," we simply learn that Satan offers an imitation of the real thing.

The Success of the New World

Look at today's industrial society. We are protected by law and order and are relatively secure. We don't have to fear driving to the mall and parking our cars. Millions do so on a daily basis. Inside the mall we see an amazing display of products for sale. Thousands of people move from store to store. Most people are very polite; they apologize when they bump into other people. Everyone is friendly and helpful. Those who belong to the 95 percent of American citizens who have jobs most likely have the money to buy what they need. They leave the shopping centers in comfortable cars and return to homes equipped with gadgets and appliances that families a couple of hundred years ago could not have even imagined owning.

Think about your neighbors, friends, relatives and the church members with whom you are acquainted. I think you would have to admit most of them are decent people who work hard to try and make life as comfortable as possible for themselves and their children. You maintain the appearance of your home and property. You go to church on Sundays, where you meet and are greeted by polite, well-dressed people. Perhaps you go to sporting events where thousands gather to root for their teams. After the games, everyone goes home and watches television programs showing how great life is and how happy people can be. So how does this behavior fulfill prophecies such as, "He shall destroy wonderfully" and "by peace shall destroy many?" The normal daily activities of good people, of decent, law-abiding, tax-paying

Those who do not believe that Jesus Christ is their Savior, the only Savior, are furthering the agenda designed by the father of lies: to lead the entire world to oppose the Lord and His Anointed.

citizens, have absolutely nothing to do with God. The world's population, with the exception of those who are born-again Christians, serves Satan. Let me make this clear: Those who do not believe that Jesus Christ is their Savior, the only Savior, are furthering the agenda designed by the father of lies to lead the entire world to oppose the Lord and His Anointed.

The World Against His Anointed

Psalm 2:1–2 summarizes civilization with these words, "Why do the heathen rage, and the people imagine a vain thing? The kings of the earth set themselves, and the rulers take counsel together, against the LORD, and against his anointed" (Psalm 2:1–2). No one is actually fighting against the Lord. In fact, the opposite is true: politicians, athletes, and even entertainers and celebrities often conclude their

147

speeches with the phrase "God bless you." Yet, the Bible makes it clear that all the world opposes the Lord and is against His Anointed. This behavior will become more obvious as time goes by, but it will not be done openly; it will be hidden. That's how Satan does "destroy wonderfully."

The Power of the Media

Consider the media and entertainment industry. Doesn't the media produce stories designed to deceive the world?

We are being indoctrinated to believe the greatest dangers are terrorism and the Middle East. But we conveniently ignore that 30–40,000 Americans are being killed each year as the result of criminal activity.

What about making gods out of humans? Every week, scores of people hand over their hard-earned money to see movie stars, or to catch a glimpse of entertainers or other celebrity. The word "idolatry" seems to be far removed from our vocabulary, yet people watch the making of idols in their own living rooms through dozens of programs designed to produce idols. Indeed, the world is ready for that one man who will be able to agree with Christians, Muslims, Hindus, Buddhists and everyone else.

He will bring peace to the Arabs and Jews and will solve the problem of global terrorism. Through his policy the world will experience unprecedented peace and prosperity. He will "by peace...destroy many."

The End of Antichrist

Verse 25 concludes, "but he shall be broken without hand." That is the exact moment when the true Prince of Peace will come to save Israel and destroy the forces of the world and the Antichrist, "whom the Lord shall consume with the spirit of his mouth, and shall destroy with the brightness of his coming" (2 Thessalonians 2:8).

"Shut Up the Vision"

After receiving this vision, Daniel was told, "And the vision of the evening and the morning which was told is true: wherefore shut thou up the vision; for it shall be for many days" (verse 26). In other words, that prophecy was not to be fulfilled until the distant future.

Chapter 9

How Prophecy Leads to Repentance

"In the first year of Darius the son of Ahasuerus, of the seed of the Medes, which was made king over the realm of the Chaldeans; In the first year of his reign I Daniel understood by books the number of the years, whereof the word of the LORD came to Jeremiah the prophet, that he would accomplish seventy years in the desolations of Jerusalem" (Daniel 9:1–2).

Daniel documented the time and name of the ruler to introduce us to this new dispensation. He believed in God and he knew the Scriptures. He recognized what Jeremiah the prophet wrote as being "the word of the LORD."

Daniel was concerned primarily with his people and the city of Jerusalem. Verse 7 relates that he humbled himself under the sins committed by Israel. Verse 11 echoes this statement: "Yea, all Israel have transgressed thy law."

What did Daniel read? Jeremiah 25:11–12, which says, "this whole land shall be a desolation, and an astonishment; and these nations shall serve the king of Babylon seventy years. And it shall come to pass, when seventy years are accomplished, that I will punish the king of Babylon, and that nation, saith the LORD, for their iniquity, and the land of the Chaldeans, and will make it perpetual desolations." Daniel took this seriously, convinced that Jerusalem would rise again after its 70–year captivity.

Daniel loved the prophetic Word. He could have just relaxed and thought, "The Word of God is true. I believe that God will bring to pass all that He has said. There is nothing I can do." But that wasn't Daniel's attitude at all. Instead, we learn from the next verse that Daniel sought the Lord by praying, by fasting, and by donning sackcloth and ashes (Daniel 9:3). His actions were unlike how we might behave. We might have Daniel anoint his head, put on his best clothes and tell his friends and fellow Jews the good news that the 70–year captivity had finally reached an end. We might think they should have prepared a great feast to celebrate the future fulfillment of the prophetic Word: Jerusalem would be set free!

Daniel the Priest

But the opposite was true: Daniel prostrated himself before the living God in sackcloth and ashes and "prayed unto the LORD my God, and made my confession, and said, O Lord, the great and dreadful God, keeping the covenant and mercy to them that love him, and to them that keep his commandments; We have sinned, and have committed iniquity, and have done wickedly, and have rebelled, even by departing from thy precepts and from thy judgments: Neither have we hearkened unto thy servants the prophets, which spake in thy name to our kings, our princes, and our fathers, and to all the people of the land. O Lord, righteousness belongeth unto thee, but unto us confusion of faces, as at this day; to the men of Judah, and to the inhabitants of Jerusalem, and unto all Israel, that are near, and that are far off, through all the countries whither thou hast driven them, because of their trespass that they have trespassed against thee" (verses 4–7).

Scripture doesn't contain any of the specific sins that Daniel may have committed. We read only about his faithfulness, dedication and resolution to serve the God of Israel: "But Daniel purposed in his heart that he would not defile himself with the portion of the king's meat, nor with the wine which he drank: therefore he requested of the prince of the eunuchs that he might not defile himself" (Daniel 1:8).

Daniel's priestly attitude was revealed in his prayer when he identified himself with the sins of his people. We read phrases such as: "We have sinned," "neither have we hearkened," "neither have we obeyed the voice of the Lord our God," and "we have done wickedly." Daniel used words like "our" and "we" instead of using words like "them" and "they."

The Law of Love

Daniel was able to include himself in this confession because he knew the God of Israel intimately. Subsequently, he became deeply burdened by the sins of his people even though technically, he was innocent. His attitude toward the sins of others fulfilled the perfect law of liberty, even 500 years before Jesus was born.

The love he had for his people was centered on the greatest of all commandments: "this is love, that we walk after his commandments. This is the commandment, That, as ye have heard from the beginning, ye should walk in it" (2 John 6).

The Apostle Paul summarized the perfect law of liberty when he wrote to the church in Galatia: "For all the law is fulfilled in one word, even in this; Thou shalt love thy neighbour as thyself" (Galatians 5:14).

That law opposes our way of thinking, our personalities, our flesh and blood. We love ourselves above all else. What a tragedy that in many of today's churches the "gospel of self-love" is promoted and even pushed upon believers.

'And hath made us kings and priests unto God and his Father' (Revelation 1:6).

We may all understand the commandment to love our neighbors as ourselves in theory, but in practice, it becomes a different story. Daniel acted according to God's Word; he practiced this love for his fellow man and was able to pray for the nation in a priestly manner.

This is a great lesson for us to learn, for we read: "And hath made us kings and priests unto God and his Father" (Revelation 1:6).

Pleading for Forgiveness

Daniel pleaded with God after he confessed: "O my God, incline thine ear, and hear; open thine eyes, and behold our desolations, and the city which is called by thy name: for we do not present our supplications before thee for our righteousnesses, but for thy great mercies. O Lord, hear; O Lord, forgive; O Lord, hearken and do; defer not, for thine own sake, O my God: for thy city and thy people are called by thy name" (Daniel 9:18–19). Not only did he plead for forgiveness, but also he reminded God of the promises He made in His Word regarding the city and the people because they were called by His name.

This is prophetically significant. We must always be mindful that when we read, hear or speak about Jerusalem and the Jewish people, we are standing on "holy ground"!

The Eternal Covenant

Jeremiah also reminded the Lord: "O LORD...we are called by thy name" (Jeremiah 14:9). He too confessed "for we have sinned against thee" (verse 20) and he continued in verse 21: "Do not abhor us, for thy name's sake, do not disgrace the throne of thy glory: remember, break not thy covenant with us." In other words, "Yes, we have sinned. Yes, we have broken the covenant, but Lord 'break not thy covenant with us.'" He knew that God had made an irreversible, eternal covenant with His people.

That is the God we serve: the God of Abraham, the God of Isaac and the God of Jacob. He is the same yesterday, today and forever. He will fulfill His prophetic Word in the exact manner He caused it to be written under the inspiration of the Holy Spirit.

No matter what the world does or how politicians and government officials act or react, Jerusalem is still His city and the Jews are still His people. Prophecies such as the ones recorded by Jeremiah will be fulfilled: "I will bring Israel again to his habitation, and he shall feed on Carmel and Bashan, and his soul shall be satisfied upon mount Ephraim and Gilead. In those days, and in that time, saith the LORD, the iniquity of Israel shall be sought for, and there shall be none; and the sins of Judah, and they shall not be found: for I will pardon them whom I reserve" (Jeremiah 50:19–20). That is Israel's hope. It is also the hope of the Church now and in the future. "The iniquity of Israel [Church] shall be sought for, and there shall be none."

Chapter **10**

THE 70 WEEKS IN PROPHECY

"And whiles I was speaking, and praying, and confessing my sin and the sin of my people Israel, and presenting my supplication before the LORD my God for the holy mountain of my God" (Daniel 9:20).

Daniel confessed the sins of his people and asked God for forgiveness. Next came the answer to Daniel's prayer: "Yea, whiles I was speaking in prayer, even the man Gabriel, whom I had seen in the vision at the beginning, being caused to fly swiftly, touched me about the time of the evening oblation. And he informed me, and talked with me, and said, O Daniel, I am now come forth to give thee skill and understanding" (verses 21–22). This angel prince was named Gabriel, a name often translated as "hero of God." Scholars have identified Gabriel as an archangel who appeared to Zecharias to announce the birth of John the Baptist and later to announce the birth of Christ to Mary. According to Luke 1:19 he came directly from the presence of God: "I am Gabriel, that stand in the presence of God."

Daniel didn't ask for wisdom, understanding or anything that would benefit himself; instead, he asked for forgiveness for the transgressions of his people.

Daniel: Our Model

Daniel serves as a fitting example of the attitude we must have when we read the prophetic Word. Prophecy is God's Word and is not of private interpretation. In other words, we can't interpret it without first meeting with the Author of prophecy: the Lord Himself. Only when we are humble and have separated from the things of this world will God give us the skill and understanding necessary for interpreting prophecy. That is why the psalmist wrote:

"The fear of the LORD is the beginning of wisdom" (Psalm 111:10).

Meeting at the Sacrifice

Notice that Gabriel appeared during the time of the evening oblation. Remember, there wasn't any temple or sacrifice at that time, yet the Bible identifies it as the time of the evening oblation. What happened during that time? The daily sacrifice — the burnt offering — was offered. This was the

This points to the greatest sacrifice, Jesus Christ, the Prophet, Priest and King — the Lamb of God in one person.

only offering presented wholly to the Lord and consumed upon the altar. This points to the greatest sacrifice, Jesus Christ, the Prophet, Priest and King –the Lamb of God in one person.

Why was Daniel preferred above all the others? The answer is found in verse 23: "for thou art greatly beloved." Daniel's love for God and His people, coupled with the realization of the sins of his people, are the reasons Daniel was greatly beloved.

The 70 Weeks

Gabriel told Daniel what would transpire: "Seventy weeks are determined upon thy people and upon thy holy city, to finish the transgression, and to make an end of sins, and to make reconciliation for iniquity, and to bring in everlasting righteousness, and to seal up the vision and prophecy, and to anoint the most Holy. Know therefore and understand, that from the going forth of the commandment to restore and to build Jerusalem unto the Messiah the Prince shall be seven weeks, and threescore and two weeks: the street shall be built again, and the wall, even in troublous times" (verses 24–25).

This prophecy spans almost 2,500 years. Daniel was told that Jerusalem and the temple would be rebuilt, but at a specific time and for a specific purpose: for the Messiah.

Let's look at several of the details:

1) To finish the transgression; 2) to make an end of sin; 3) to make reconciliation for iniquity; 4) to usher in everlasting righteousness; 5) to seal up the vision of prophecy; 6) to anoint the most holy.

We will look at several other translations to get the bigger picture contained in this important verse: "Seventy sevens are decreed for your people and your holy city to finish transgression, to put an end to sin, to atone for wickedness, to bring in everlasting righteousness, to seal up vision and prophecy and to anoint the most holy" (Daniel 9:24– NIV). The German Schlachter version says: "Seventy weeks have been determined over your people and the holy city to fulfill the measure of transgression and to fill the measure of sin to make atonement for wickedness, to bring forth eternal righteousness and to confirm the visions of the prophets and to anoint the high holy one." According to my understanding of this passage, this verse extends from the Babylonian captivity to the anointing of the Holy One.

1. The 70-year captivity completed the transgression. Daniel prayed about it, confessed it and asked for forgiveness.

2. To make an end to sin, which included the idolatry that was practiced by Israel until they were taken captive.

3. It included reconciliation or atonement for iniquity.

4. The result would be "to bring in everlasting righteousness." On one hand, these things are written about the nation of Israel, but on the other, they are written about the Messiah, for there is no one but Jesus who can put an end to sin, bring about reconciliation or create an everlasting righteousness.

5. The phrases "seal up the vision of prophecy" and "prophetic visions ratified" remind us of Matthew's Gospel account, which emphasizes the fulfillment of the Old Covenant: "Now all this was done, that it might be fulfilled which was spoken of the Lord by the prophet" (Matthew 1:22). "And was there until the death of Herod: that it might be fulfilled which was spoken of the Lord by the prophet, saying, Out of Egypt have I called my son...Then was fulfilled that which was spoken by Jeremy the prophet, saying...And he came and dwelt in a city called Nazareth: that it might be fulfilled which was spoken by the prophets, He shall be called a Nazarene" (Matthew 2:15,17,23).

6. Long before Daniel, the prophet Isaiah wrote about the anointment: "The Spirit of the Lord GOD is upon me; because the LORD hath anointed me to preach good tidings unto the meek; he hath sent me to bind up the brokenhearted, to proclaim liberty to the captives, and the opening of the prison to them that are bound; To proclaim the acceptable year of the LORD, and the day of vengeance of our God; to comfort all that mourn" (Isaiah 61:1–2). Fulfilled in Luke 4:18, the Lord stated in verse 21: "This day is this scripture fulfilled in your ears."

The Exact Time

Even an exact time is provided: "seven weeks, and threescore and two weeks," or 69 weeks. Daniel understood a week to mean seven years, which is not an unusual occurrence in Scripture. For example, Jacob worked for Laban seven years in order to receive Rachel's hand in marriage. According to Genesis 29, Uncle Laban tricked Jacob by offering Leah's hand in marriage instead of Rachel. When Jacob objected, Laban told him, "Fulfil her week…which thou shalt serve with me yet seven other years" (Genesis 29:27).

Some scholars have figured Jesus' death to the very day according to the timetable recorded in Scripture. This obviously requires an extensive amount of study on the subject. But suffice it to say, the Messiah came, and according to the introductory Scripture, He died: "shall Messiah be cut off." The Tanakh says: "And after those 62 weeks, the anointed one will disappear and vanish."

According to the Gospel accounts, Jesus' role as Israel's Messiah was suspended after He was crucified. But He became "the first begotten of the dead." God did a new work: "For God so loved the world, that he gave his only begotten Son, that whosoever believeth in him should not perish, but have everlasting life" (John 3:16).

These facts are recorded in Scripture and a number of other historic writings. Jesus came to this earth to fulfill the work His Father sent Him here to accomplish.

In 70 A.D. "the prince that shall come shall destroy the city and the sanctuary." Therefore, this prophecy covers the rebuilding of Jerusalem and the temple; the coming of the Messiah; His death; the destruction of Jerusalem and the tem-

Jesus came to this earth to fulfill the work His Father sent Him here to accomplish.

ple; then an undisclosed time when "the anointed one will disappear and vanish" and ultimately the "overspreading of abominations."

When Will the Abomination Take Place?

When will this empty space of time end for Israel? When the Antichrist "confirm(s) the covenant." Verse 27 says, "And he shall confirm the covenant with many for one week: and in the midst of the week he shall cause the sacrifice and the oblation to cease, and for the overspreading of abominations he shall make it desolate, even until the consummation, and that determined shall be poured upon the desolate."

A number of theories exist regarding what type of covenant this will be. One of the most popular views is that the European Union will sign a peace covenant with Israel, thus guaranteeing its existence. While this does seem to make sense, I am not fully convinced that such will be the case, therefore, we must simply leave this important statement without any further explanation: "he shall confirm the covenant with many for one week." A covenant with Israel will be established for one week (seven years), at which time the temple will be rebuilt. This will be necessary because the Antichrist must put an end to the sacrifices. Second Thessalonians 2:4 says: "Who opposeth and exalteth himself above all that is called God, or that is worshipped; so that he as God sitteth in the temple of God, shewing himself that he is God."

Progress Toward Fulfillment

Preparation for the fulfillment of these prophecies was impossible only a mere 100 years ago because there was no Israel and the Jews were scattered throughout the world. The Jews have a homeland today. Although their residence is contested by the nations, they are nevertheless a nation. Israel has become a stumbling stone for the rest of the world.

For the first time in human history, we see a nation stand alone, opposed by the rest of the world. I have often made this statement and must repeat it again here: No nation agrees to the borders God ordained for Israel from the Euphrates River to the river of Egypt.

Now, some may say this is a "religious" issue that does not apply to the politics and geography of today. Let's assume that is the case. We can agree that the establish-

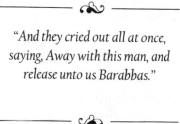

"And they cried out all at once, saying, Away with this man, and release unto us Barabbas."

ment of every nation has been the result of the use of force, with winners establishing the borders of their countries. But the rules have changed for Israel, which conquered significant portions of Promised Land territory in four major wars. Even though they won those wars, they were pressured by the United States to withdraw from the conquered territories and surrender them to those who had sworn the destruction of Israel.

Is history repeating itself? Pontius Pilate asked the Jewish people whether he should release Jesus or Barabbas: "And they cried out all at once, saying, Away with this man, and release unto us Barabbas" (Luke 23:18). When given the choice — "shall I crucify your king?" — they replied, "We have no king but Caesar" (John 19:15).

Today's Situation

The world voices its opinions about Israel. Instead of siding with Israel, it favors Arafat and his henchmen. Arab terrorists are not being held accountable for murdering Jews. We must not become confused by temporary political circumstances. The prophetic Word is forever; the actions or statements made by any leader will not change that. The prophetic Word will not change regardless of whether we support Israel. The fact remains that all the nations will oppose Israel. The president of the United States cannot change Scripture. He is obligated by the powers of darkness to oppose Israel, particularly Jerusalem. It is impossible for any president to declare Jerusalem the indivisible capital city of Israel. Even if a president did acknowledge the "Jewishness" of Jerusalem, the rest of the world certainly would not agree. All nations must follow the invisible dictates of the prince of darkness, the god of this world. These are truly the end stages of the endtimes. Jesus is coming soon!

Chapter **11**

ISRAEL'S TRIBULATION AND REDEMPTION

"In the third year of Cyrus king of Persia a thing was revealed unto Daniel, whose name was called Belteshazzar; and the thing was true, but the time appointed was long: and he understood the thing, and had understanding of the vision. In those days I Daniel was mourning three full weeks. I ate no pleasant bread, neither came flesh nor wine in my mouth, neither did I anoint myself at all, till three whole weeks were fulfilled. And in the four and twentieth day of the first month, as I was by the side of the great river, which is Hiddekel" (Daniel 10:1–4).

Preparation To Receive

Daniel's fourth vision was about the Great Tribulation, the Jewish people and the world.

This vision wasn't received while he fasted, but after he had fasted for three weeks. During this fast he denied himself of "pleasant bread." The Tanakh uses the English words "tasty food." Neither did Daniel eat any meat or drink any wine — two substances that contribute to one's fleshly self-confidence. In fact, drinking wine tends to cause a person to overestimate himself.

Scripture also explains that Daniel did nothing about his appearance, which naturally would have boosted his self-confidence: "neither did I anoint myself at all." From this description we learn that receiving spiritual knowledge requires certain preparation. Apparently self-denial is the key.

The Euphrates River

Daniel identified the day and the place where this occurred: "in the four and twentieth day of the first month, as I was by the side of the great river, which is Hiddekel" (verse 4). Hiddekel is also known as the Tigris, the river mentioned in the Garden of Eden description. The Tigris and Euphrates rivers begin in the mountains of Armenia and flow down for almost 1,760 km (1,100 miles), meeting in the Persian Gulf.

The Euphrates River is popularly mentioned in conjunction with the endtimes in relation to the Great Tribulation and the Battle of Armageddon. Daniel's fourth and final vision illustrates the beginning and the end: the Garden of Eden and Armageddon.

Daniel's third vision of the 70 weeks is recorded in chapter 9. That was in the first year of Chaldean King Darius.

The second vision took place at "the river of Elah," which some scholars believe is located in Shushan. *Unger's Bible Dictionary* says: "It was... the place of Daniel's vision under Belshazzar."

Chapter 7 contains the record of the first vision, which shows the four Gentile power structures represented by three animals and a beast.

The Fourth Vision

This vision apparently had taken place in Daniel's new homeland, Babylon. It is helpful to read the entire book of Daniel in one sitting and then to read the book of Revelation immediately thereafter. That's a great way to get a clear picture of the endtimes for Israel as a nation, Jerusalem as the capital, the Church residing in the heavenly Jerusalem and the future of the Gentile world.

Here at the Hiddekel River, Daniel saw a man and described him in detail: "Then I lifted up mine eyes, and looked, and behold a certain man clothed in linen, whose loins were girded with fine gold of Uphaz: His body also was like the beryl, and his face as the appearance of lightning, and his eyes as lamps of fire, and his arms and his feet like in colour to polished brass, and the voice of his words like the voice of a multitude" (Daniel 10:5–6). This is unquestionably the Lord, for

Revelation 1:13–15 says: "And in the midst of the seven candlesticks one like unto the Son of man, clothed with a garment down to the foot, and girt about the paps with a golden girdle. His head and his hairs were white like wool, as white as snow; and his eyes were as a flame of fire; And his feet like unto fine brass, as if they burned in a furnace; and his voice as the sound of many waters."

The Beginning and End of Grace

There is, however, a distinct difference. Daniel reported that his "loins were girded with fine gold of Uphaz." John the Revelator wrote that the Lord was "girt about the paps with a golden girdle." Important to understand is that in Daniel's vision, the Lord was ready to do the task that the Father had entrusted to Him. But in the book of Revelation, this golden girdle was around His chest, signifying that the work had already been done. John reveals that the chest–that is, the location of the heart — is covered. He no longer is the servant, but has become the Judge, the King of kings and Lord of lords. The time of grace will have expired.

A Message for Israel

The reason for Daniel's prayer and the answer are clearly stated: "What shall befall thy people in the latter days?" Nothing is mentioned about the Gentiles.

Another Jew revealed the message to the Gentiles, a Benjaminite named Saul. Acts 9:3–4 says: "And as he journeyed, he came near Damascus: and suddenly there shined round about him a light from heaven: And he fell to the earth, and heard a voice saying unto him, Saul, Saul, why persecutest thou me?" Saul asked: "Lord, what wilt thou have me to do?" (Acts 9:6). What was Saul's calling? "For he is a chosen vessel unto me, to bear my name before the Gentiles, and kings, and the children of Israel" (Acts 9:15). Israel is not the key here; in fact, it is mentioned last. In spite of the fact that the Gentile nations do not have a future, God has mercifully opened the door for the Gospel message to be preached. We have been invited to become a part of the great multitude of people who are saved by the blood of the Lamb. This salvation is not available for nations collectively but only on an individual basis.

This salvation is not available for nations collectively but only on an individual basis.

In Daniel's case, the people who were with him "saw not the vision...they fled to hide themselves." Daniel's message was for the future, for the times of the end. For that reason he was later instructed to "Shut up the words and seal the book, even to the time of the end."

What a merciful God we serve! He is full of grace and truth, and desires that we understand His Word, especially now in the end stages of the endtimes when chaos reigns and the Bible is too often used as a cleverly manipulated commercial product. But each one of us is responsible to search the Scriptures for ourselves. We are to seek the Lord's countenance and do as Daniel. Only then can the Lord pronounce these wonderful words about our lives: "Thou art greatly beloved."

Heavenly Messengers

Daniel was overwhelmed by a vision he received in the third year of the reign of Persian King Cyrus, when he saw a man who turned out to be none other than the Son of God.

Daniel became powerless in His awesome presence: "And I Daniel alone saw the vision: for the men that were with me saw not the vision; but a great quaking fell upon them, so that they fled to hide themselves. Therefore I was left alone, and saw this great vision, and there remained no strength in me: for my comeliness was turned in me into corruption, and I retained no strength. Yet heard I the voice of his words: and when I heard the voice of his words, then was I in a deep sleep on my face, and my face toward the ground" (Daniel 10:7–9). This is the Word of God and again, Daniel fell into a "deep sleep," which Luther translated as a period when he was "unconscious" or "powerless."

In this condition and at that moment, "behold, an hand touched me, which set me upon my knees and upon the palms of my hands" (verse 10). We don't read whose hand it was, but we know it wasn't the Lord's; it was the messenger's. The touch "...set me upon my knees and upon the palms of my hands."

174

Greatly Beloved

Then something marvelous happened: "he said unto me, O Daniel, a man greatly beloved, understand the words that I speak unto thee, and stand upright: for unto thee am I now sent. And when he had spoken this word unto me, I stood trembling" (verse 11). Daniel received the wonderful

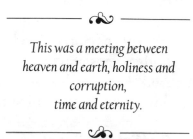

This was a meeting between heaven and earth, holiness and corruption, time and eternity.

testimony that he was greatly beloved and then he was ordered to understand the words "while standing upright." Why was that necessary? Because his entire being — spirit, soul and body — had to be made capable of receiving the heavenly message, which concerned the earth and its people, particularly the Jews.

Daniel was not permitted to lie down or even to sit; he had to stand up and receive the message while he was fully conscious and had all of his faculties in tact.

We mustn't forget that this was a meeting between heaven and earth, holiness and corruption, time and eternity.

Another reason for Daniel's having to stand was that a heavenly messenger was in his presence—not unlike our custom today of rising in honor of a judge when he enters the courtroom.

Daniel was called "greatly beloved" from a heavenly perspective but from an earthly perspective he had no power or strength; he testified that he "stood trembling."

Then came the message: "Then said he unto me, Fear not, Daniel: for from the first day that thou didst set thine heart to understand, and to chasten thyself before thy God, thy words were heard, and I am come for thy words" (verse 12). Daniel's prayer initiated the appearance of the Son of God: "I am come for thy words." Luther translates this as: "I have come for your sakes." And the Tenakh says: "Your prayer was heard and I have come because of your prayer."

Our Solemn Duty

If only we could even remotely understand the tremendous power of prayer: Heaven and hell are moved. Why don't we pray more often? Prayer, not protest, is the most effective type of warfare we can possibly wage. Of course, we would rather sign petitions; however, the only actions we can take that give the devil problems are when we, the saints, kneel in prayer.

Dear child of God, when you act on the impulse to pray quickly so that you can take care of other things, then you have failed to persevere in the Lord. It is when we do not feel like praying that we should cry out to God. Many servants of God can attest that the more we pray, the more time we seem to have and the more we can accomplish. The less we pray, the more overwhelmed we become and soon it seems that we haven't any time to pray. That is the devil's goal. Notice

Prayer, not protest, is the most effective type of warfare we can possibly wage.

also that Daniel had no support in this situation, but testified in verse 8: "I was left alone."

The Conflict

Now the conflict between heaven and hell, between God and Satan, is revealed. Let us read verses 12–13 once again: "Then said he unto me, Fear not, Daniel: for from the first day that thou didst set thine heart to understand, and to chasten thyself before thy God, thy words were heard, and I am come for thy words. But the prince of the kingdom of Persia withstood me one and twenty days: but, lo, Michael, one of the chief princes, came to help me; and I remained there with the kings of Persia."

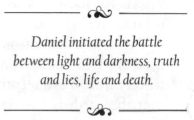

Daniel initiated the battle between light and darkness, truth and lies, life and death.

This battle in the invisible world began the moment Daniel started to pray: "from the first day that thou didst set thine heart to understand" Thus, Daniel initiated the battle between light and darkness, truth and lies, life and death.

Who is the Prince of Persia?

Who are the enemies? "The prince of the kingdom of Persia." Are we to assume this prince was one of the princes of Persia's King Cyrus? Obviously not, because when Daniel wrote that he was alone when he saw the vision, we must understand that we are sent into the spiritual realm.

Daniel was a great adviser to the king of Persia, who had significant political power; therefore, the prince of Persia was not an actual person but a powerful prince of the demonic world. Here we are concerned with spiritual things, which must obviously be spiritually discerned.

Daniel was literally and physically in the kingdom of Persia. The location was given as "the great river, which is Hiddekel" (Tigris).

This vision came from heaven, but in order for the messenger to come from heaven to earth, he had to travel through evil territory. I think we would all agree that the earth is the devil's territory. The Bible says about humanity: "There is none righteous, no, not one" (Romans 3:10).

Spiritual Battle

The Apostle Paul revealed this spiritual battle to the believers when he wrote: "For we wrestle not against flesh and blood, but against principalities, against powers, against the rulers of the darkness of this world, against spiritual wickedness in high places" (Ephesians 6:12). It becomes clear yet again that our battle is not against things that can be physically identified. It is not against the evil, unrighteous and immoral people of this world; it is against the powers of darkness that stand behind these people. Luther offers a more concise translation: "against...the evil spirits under the heaven."

Planet Earth is demonized; it is surrounded by the powers of darkness. This earth is ruled by the god of this world, the prince of darkness, because we all have sinned and we all fall short of the glory of God (Romans 3:23), and "He that committeth sin is of the devil; for the devil sinneth from the beginning" (1 John 3:8).

This verse contradicts the frequently misused expression, "We all are children of God." According to 1 John 3:8, we are children of Satan. With this in mind, we have exposed Satan's religious activity, which he uses to ensnare millions of Christians around the world. It comes under the pretext of nationalism or patriotism: "One nation under God" and "In God we trust." These phrases refer to the god of this world, not Jesus Christ.

But thanks to God He has provided a way of escape through Jesus, who is the Door, the Life, and the Truth, and in whom no darkness is found. We become born again children of God when we place our faith in Him and what He did for us on Calvary's cross.

A cloud of demonic powers surrounds this world. People and governments, regardless of the type, are subject to the prince of the air, "spiritual wickedness in high places."

But that fact doesn't change God's sovereignty; He is above all things. Even Satan and his host of demons can only go as far as God will allow; otherwise, we would literally experience hell on earth. The fact that we can exist as Christians on planet Earth is nothing less than God's grace, which He extends to us through Jesus Christ, the great Advocate and our High Priest.

Michael to the Rescue

Opposition in the invisible world is so powerful that this heavenly messenger needed reinforcement: "But lo, Michael, one of the chief princes, came to help me; and I remained there with the kings of Persia" (Daniel 10:13). Notice again the word "kings" is plural. This is Satan's power structure and his angelic host, which insists that planet Earth and all it contains belongs to Satan. They demanded their rights against Daniel's prayer by the subsequent response to his prayer: the appearance of the heavenly messenger.

Who is this Michael? He is the only one who is identified in Scripture as an archangel. "Yet Michael the archangel, when contending with the devil he disputed about the body of Moses, durst not bring against him a railing accusation, but said, The Lord rebuke" (Jude 9). What a tremendous revelation! Moses' body became a subject of contention between the devil and Michael the archangel. Even Michael the archangel did not condemn the devil, but said: "The Lord rebuke thee." In other words, it wasn't Michael's job to condemn the devil because that task is reserved for God, the righteous Judge.

The German Menge translation says: "But the guardian angel of the Persian Empire opposed me for 21 days." The hidden truths behind nationalism and patriotism are exposed when we grasp this tremendous statement. The motto "For God and country" sounds pretty shallow when it is analyzed from a heavenly perspective.

180

The Latter Days

All of this was in preparation for the information Daniel was about to receive regarding the Jews: "Now I am come to make thee understand what shall befall thy people in the latter days: for yet the vision is for many days" (verse 14).

These few words caused Daniel to faint again: "And when he had spoken such words unto me, I set my face toward the ground, and I became dumb" (verse 15). Daniel needed to be strengthened again: "And, behold, one like the similitude of the sons of men touched my lips: then I opened my mouth, and spake, and said unto him that stood before me." Then he had just enough strength to speak: "O my lord, by the vision my sorrows are turned upon me, and I have retained no strength. For how can the servant of this my lord talk with this my lord? For as for me, straightway there remained no strength in me, neither is there breath left in me" (verses 16b–17). Once again, Daniel had to be strengthened: "Then there came again and touched me one like the appearance of a man, and he strengthened me" (verse 18).

What an encouragement it must have been for Daniel to hear the words: "O man greatly beloved" (verse 19). Then he was instructed to "be strong, yea, be strong." And he confessed, "And when he had spoken unto me, I was strengthened, and said, Let my lord speak; for thou hast strengthened me" (verse 19).

The Future

"Then said he, Knowest thou wherefore I come unto thee? And now will I return to fight with the prince of Persia: and when I am gone forth, lo, the prince of Grecia shall come" This verse clearly reveals that the battle continues in the invisible world between the powers of God and the powers of Satan and the nations.

God is not against the nations per se; the Bible says He loved the world so much that He gave His only begotten Son. But we are concerned here with the demonic world, the fallen angels, Satan himself, who opposes God. Satan has a legal right to all the nations of the world. God, however, has the upper hand and allows the devil to execute his diabolical plan only as far as the limits He sets. One thing becomes clear: Satan has deceived the nations; they do his bidding. They refuse to come to Jesus and receive forgiveness of their sins. Instead, they serve the father of lies, making themselves servants of Satan.

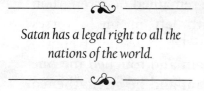

Satan has a legal right to all the nations of the world.

All Have Sinned

It makes no difference whether you are a Christian, Muslim, Hindu or atheist — the devil has no problem with the sinful world. The Bible says that he who sins is of the devil (1 John 3:8), giving him the legal right to every sinner.

God's problem is really with each individual's refusal

to accept the only way out of this demonized world into true freedom now and for all eternity.

It's not the kind of freedom obtained by military force. Those pipe dreams are being spread throughout the world. During my recent travels to various countries, I was amazed by the number of statues, memorials and victory arches dedicated to soldiers who had "lain down their lives" for the freedom of their nations. I strongly disagree with this sentiment. The only One who has laid down His life is Jesus Christ. Any soldier who has been killed during battle has not laid down his life, but his life has been taken from him because he tried to take another man's life.

Let us never insult God's eternal plan of salvation by assuming we have somehow received freedom by force. That's the devil's message — the father of lies has been a murderer from day one.

Michael's Help for Israel

The center of the heavenly message, however, is directed to the Jews, God's connection between heaven and earth: "But I will shew thee that which is noted in the Scripture of truth: and there is none

The only One who has laid down His life is Jesus Christ.

that holdeth with me in these things, but Michael your prince" (verse 21).

The fact is again revealed that Michael the archangel stands for the children of Israel and opposes the nations of the world regardless of their form of government.

A New Age theology has been established categorizing all of Israel's present enemies and creating a camp of "them" and "us." But that is not what the Bible says. Israel is one nation against the world; that is what the Bible teaches.

Michael, the prince of Israel, will interfere on Israel's behalf when the Rapture takes place: "For the Lord himself shall descend from heaven with a shout, with the voice of the archangel, and with the trump of God: and the dead in Christ shall rise first" (1 Thessalonians 4:16). Here we have the word "archangel" and although no name is mentioned, it seems logical that it is Michael who, with a loud voice, will call, "come up hither." He will come down to earth ready to stand for the children of Israel.

We must not overlook that there will be a terrible void on earth when the Church of Jesus Christ has been raptured. The light of the world will be gone, the salt of the earth will have disappeared and countless angels, which minister to the saints, as Hebrews 1:14 indicates, will have disappeared: "Are they not all ministering spirits, sent forth to minister for them who shall be heirs of salvation?" The time for the Great Tribulation will have begun!

Chapter 12

THE POWERS UNDER HEAVEN

"Also I in the first year of Darius the Mede, even I, stood to confirm and to strengthen him. And now will I shew thee the truth. Behold, there shall stand up yet three kings in Persia; and the fourth shall be far richer than they all: and by his strength through his riches he shall stir up all against the realm of Grecia. And a mighty king shall stand up, that shall rule with great dominion, and do according to his will" (Daniel 11:1–3).

Daniel continued to receive the fourth and final vision. He saw the powers of darkness that rule this world and oppose the powers of light, which come from God's presence.

This nameless man came to deliver a message to Daniel concerning his people, the Jews.

In the previous chapter we learned that Michael, one of the chief princes of the angelic heavenly host, had defended this heavenly messenger "and there is none that holdeth with me in these things, but Michael your prince" (Daniel 10:21). I don't believe it is necessary to speculate about the identity of this heavenly messenger. Obviously there is a reason his identity is not revealed and we should leave it at that.

Michael helped the messenger, but as chapter 11 begins, we learn that the messenger also helped Michael: "Also I in the first year of Darius the Mede, even I, stood to confirm and to strengthen him." Another translation reads: "During Darius the Mede, first year as king, I strengthened and defended Michael." Although several other translations seem to indicate that this angelic host was helping strengthen King Darius, I am inclined to believe this heavenly messenger received help from Michael and Michael received help from him. We must keep in mind that this is a heavenly vision, one that leads us into the invisible world where we see a collision between God's angelic host and the evil empire, the devil and his angels. Whenever King Darius, Media-Persia or Babylon are mentioned, it's the result of preceding events that took place in the invisible world.

Angels, Not Dictators

Angels cannot impose dictatorial power and assert themselves at their will. Jesus prayed, "Father, if thou be willing, remove this cup from me: nevertheless, not my will, but thine, be done," then "there appeared an angel unto him from heaven, strengthening him" (Luke 22:42-43). Why was Jesus weak in the face of the enemy? "Wherefore in all things it behoved him to be made like unto his brethren, that he might be a merciful and faithful high priest in things pertaining to God, to make reconciliation for the sins of the people. For in that he himself hath suffered being tempted, he is able to succour them that are tempted" (Hebrews 2:17–18). The angel could not come to strengthen Jesus before He had declared His willingness to die then and there.

Did Jesus Pray To Avoid the Cross?

Hebrews 5:7 says: "Who in the days of his flesh, when he had offered up prayers and supplications with strong crying and tears unto him that was able to save him from death, and was heard in that he feared." This explains Jesus' prayer in the Garden: "O my Father, if it be possible, let this cup pass from me: nevertheless not as I will, but as thou wilt" (Matthew 26:39). Here we have the revelation that Jesus did not pray for His life to be spared on the cross, but He prayed that His life would be spared right there in the Garden of Gethsemane. Before He prayed, He said: "My soul is exceeding sorrowful, even unto death" (Matthew 26:38). All of death and of hell was laid upon Jesus in the Garden of Gethsemane so that He shed sweat that was "as it were great drops of blood." Doubtless He was near death. Had He died in the Garden of Gethsemane He wouldn't have carried away the sins of the world on the cross and prophecy would not have been fulfilled. Hebrews 5:7 reveals that God heard and answered His prayer. God did save Him from death;

God did save Him from death; Jesus did not die in the Garden of Gethsemane.

Jesus did not die in the Garden of Gethsemane but He went on to fulfill prophecy by dying on the cross in Golgatha.

The Devil's Right to Sinners

Since the devil is the father of lies and all have sinned, all are of the devil; therefore, the demonic powers have a legal right to contest God's decision to implement grace.

In Daniel's case, the demonic forces opposed the heavenly messenger because he was about to proclaim Israel's salvation.

Incidentally, that message is not only opposed by the demonic world but by the majority of Churchianity. It is not popular to preach scriptural judgment to the world, nor is it popular to speak about the return of Jesus because most members of Churchianity believe they deserve more luxurious lives. The imminency of the Lord's return is an uncomfortable message that interferes with their plans.

Moses was a great man of God who presented the law to his people, but he was still a sinner. Thus, Jude 1:9 says: "Yet Michael the archangel, when contending with the devil he disputed about the body of Moses, durst not bring against him a railing accusation, but said, The Lord rebuke thee." In other words, the devil was saying: "This body is mine, it's sinful; its flesh and blood." Yet

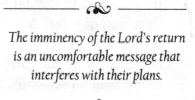

The imminency of the Lord's return is an uncomfortable message that interferes with their plans.

God overruled him. This overruling is not natural nor is it deserving; it is an act of grace beyond our ability to comprehend.

The Devil Knows Prophecy

An amazing volume of information is available about the kings of the North and the South. Egypt lies to the south of Israel while Syria, Turkey and Russia are located to the north. However, all this information relates to the key of the information package: "I am come to make thee understand what shall befall thy people in the latter days" (Daniel 10:14).

189

The devil knew the One who would crush the serpent's head would come from the line of Judah. Jesus said salvation is of the Jews. This salvation wouldn't be established by brute force or by supernatural power, but by an act of sacrifice.

The devil knows Scripture and the prophetic Word, but he doesn't know exactly when or how God will defeat him.

Let's consider an example of the devil's knowledge in Matthew 8, when Jesus met two demon-possessed men at Gergesenes. When the men saw Jesus coming, they protested: "What have we to do with thee, Jesus, thou Son of God? Art thou come hither to torment us before the time?" (verse 29). This shows that the demons knew the prophetic Word and the approximate timetable; thus, they protested against His intention to exhibit His authority to cast out demons.

Jesus Fulfilled Prophecy

Jesus came to Israel to establish God's kingdom on earth. His first sermon contained only nine words: "Repent: for the kingdom of heaven is at hand" (Matthew 4:17). In order to show the people that the King had arrived to establish the kingdom, He had to fulfill Isaiah 61:1–2: "The Spirit of the Lord GOD is upon me; because the LORD hath anointed me to preach good tidings unto the meek; he hath sent me to bind up the brokenhearted, to proclaim liberty to the captives, and the opening of the prison to them that are bound; To proclaim the acceptable year of the LORD, and the day of vengeance of our God; to comfort all that mourn."

Restoration had to take place with the coming of the Messiah. The Jews were supposed to believe the signs Jesus performed by the power of God, but they didn't.

The Third Gentile Superpower

At the time of the vision Daniel had already experienced Babylon and served in Persia. But the conflict with the Gentile world continued with Greece, the next superpower recorded in verse 2: "And now will I shew thee the truth. Behold, there shall stand up yet three kings in Persia; and the fourth shall be far richer than they all: and by his strength through his riches he shall stir up all against the realm of Grecia."

To do one's own will is to do the will of the flesh, which is ruled by the devil.

Then we read that this mighty king "shall stand up, that shall rule with great dominion, and do according to his will" (Daniel 11:3). This is not the Antichrist, but clearly is one of his many forerunners.

To do one's own will is to do the will of the flesh, which is ruled by the devil. It is relatively clear that this is referring to Alexander the Great, whose mighty kingdom extended from the Black Sea to the south of Egypt and from Libya in the west to India in the east:

"And when he shall stand up, his kingdom shall be broken, and shall be divided toward the four winds of heaven; and not to his posterity, nor according to his dominion which he ruled: for his kingdom shall be plucked up, even for others beside those" (verse 4). History records that Alexander the Great was suddenly "broken" and his mighty empire was "divided towards the four winds of heaven." This was fulfilled when his kingdom was divided among his four generals.

And the conflict continues: Wars and rumors of wars are just as numerous as they were 2,500 years ago.

Forerunners of Antichrist

The king who does "according to his will" will not last; "his kingdom shall be plucked up." Then there is an attempt for peace: "And in the end of years they shall join themselves together; for the king's daughter of the south shall come to the king of the north to make an agreement: but she shall not retain the power of the arm; neither shall he stand, nor his arm: but she shall be given up, and they that brought her, and he that begat her, and he that strengthened her in these times" (verse 6). This won't result in peace either, because the Bible says that, "she shall be given up."

Then comes another strong one: "But out of a branch of her roots shall one stand up in his estate, which shall come with an army, and shall enter into

192

the fortress of the king of the north, and shall deal against them, and shall prevail: And shall also carry captives into Egypt their gods, with their princes, and with their precious vessels of silver and of gold; and he shall continue more years than the king of the north. So the king of the south shall come into his kingdom, and shall return into his own land" (verses 7–9).

Israel is located between the north and south, although it is not actively involved in the vision at this point. Daniel, however, was specifically told that this vision was "to make thee understand what shall befall thy people in the latter days." Therefore, Israel has always been the key in relationship to the nations of the world.

The progression of these events reveals the characteristics of the powers of this world in opposition to the characteristics of God's power. Verse 12 says: "And when he hath taken away the multitude, his heart shall be lifted up; and he shall cast down many ten thousands: but he shall not be strengthened by it." Again, that will not lead him anywhere despite his amazing victory and demonstration of power: "He shall cast down many ten thousands."

A notable point is revealed in verse 14: "The robbers of thy people shall exalt themselves to establish the vision; but they shall fall." The German Menge translation makes it even clearer: "During those times many shall rebel against the king of the south, even from your people among the powerful ones will join to fulfill the vision but they will fall." This obviously concerns the Jews who joined the rebellious forces in order to establish their own power base.

Down to Earth

We return to earth beginning in verse 16. What does that mean? As we previously mentioned, Daniel received a vision that came from heaven, thus it must be understood from a heavenly perspective. Although many scholars believe the kings of the north and south can be identified, I would rather not speculate because the Bible doesn't provide the names. However, the story takes a turn in verse 16: "But he that cometh against him shall do according to his own will, and none shall stand before him: and he shall stand in the glorious land, which by his hand shall be consumed." The "glorious land" no doubt refers to Israel. The visible manifestation between God and man was established in and through Israel. The battle between light and darkness was visibly manifested in this land when Jesus, nailed to the cross and bleeding to death, cried out, "It is finished!" The collision was made visible. We also note the words "shall do according to his own will."

The "glorious land" no doubt refers to Israel.

I Will...I Will...I Will

The spirit of Antichrist stands opposed to the God

of heaven by attempting to fulfill his own will.

Isaiah 14:13–14 comes to mind: "For thou hast said in thine heart, I will ascend into heaven, I will exalt my throne above the stars of God: I will sit also upon the mount of the congregation, in the sides of the north: I will ascend above the heights of the clouds; I will be like the most High." Satan's will is not God's will.

Another Loser

We learned in verse 14 that some of Israel's powerful people joined the rebellion. The defeat is recorded in verse 15: "and the arms of the south shall not withstand, neither his chosen people, neither shall there be any strength to withstand." In the end we see his fall too: "Then he shall turn his face toward the fort of his own land: but he shall stumble and fall, and not be found" (Daniel 11:19).

The Tax Man Cometh

Verse 20 introduces us to another ruler: "Then shall stand up in his estate a raiser of taxes in the glory of the kingdom: but within few days he shall be destroyed, neither in anger, nor in battle" (verse 20).

We are all too familiar with terms like "tax" and "taxation." Bible scholars tend to differ in their opinions about the kind of taxes to which this passage refers, but one thing is clear: Taxes of any type are always directed towards people. A person's name, address and location of property are necessary to assess taxes. The system of taxation is practiced in societies around the globe. Even the Israelites, who existed under God's direct authority, were instructed to pay taxes (tithes) to the governing system, a political and religious infrastructure.

We have become so accustomed to taxation that we don't even realize owning private property has become a thing of the past: The government can take away our houses if we do not pay our taxes.

But this "raiser of taxes" vanishes and "within a few days he shall be destroyed." For the sake of clarity, it may be helpful to quote from the Tanakh: "his places will be taken by one who will dispatch an office to exact tribute for royal glory, but he will be broken in a few days, not by wrath or by war."

Refined Politician

Next in line comes someone who resembles the coming Antichrist in even finer detail. Notice the words "peaceably," "flatteries," "league," and "deceitfully." "In his estate shall stand up a vile person, to whom they shall not give the honour of the kingdom: but he shall come in peaceably, and obtain the kingdom by flatteries. And with the arms of a flood shall they be overflown from before him, and shall be broken; yea, also the prince of the covenant. And after the league made with him he shall work deceitfully: for he shall come up, and shall become strong with a small people" (verses 21–23).

This sounds just like democracy. How do people

get elected to office in the government these days? Those who are elected must demonstrate peace, use flatteries, make a league, or join with others, and practice deceit.

This is extremely difficult to accomplish, but therein lies the art of politics. A successful politician always presents himself as peace-loving. Notice that politicians are often photographed kissing babies. No one wants to elect a person whose intention is to go to war.

Flattery is the art of using words that touch the heart of listeners and play on their emotions. People will believe in those who can accomplish this.

Next comes the league, which is absolutely necessary in an election. The candidate must win over the endorsement of various groups: "If you do this for me I'll do that for you." Here we read about the prince of the covenant and the league made with him, which indicates negotiated progress.

Even today candidates promise to deliver the moon and the stars, but once elected, they don't feel obligated to keep their word because they can follow their own agenda.

If you want to know what deceit is, just read some of the political campaign slogans. Remarkably, they don't tell blatant lies; they cleverly manipulate the facts and mix them with fantasy. As a result, they reach the goal of "becom[ing] strong with a small people."

Victory by Treason

This leader's march of victory continues: "He shall enter peaceably even upon the fattest places of the province; and he shall do that which his fathers have not done, nor his fathers' fathers; he shall scatter among them the prey, and spoil, and riches: yea, and he shall forecast his devices against the strong holds, even for a time" (Daniel 11:24). Again, note the words "peaceably" and "forecast...devices." This vile individual comes in the name of peace but destroys the opposition. Doesn't that sound like a dictator?

Those who have reached a critical point of power must solidify their authority. This "vile" person does it cleverly. The nameless enemy, the king of the South, is being defeated by treason: "Yea, they that feed of the portion of his meat shall destroy him, and his army shall overflow: and many shall fall down slain. And both these kings' hearts shall be to do mischief, and they shall speak lies at one table; but it shall not prosper: for yet the end shall be at the time appointed" (verses 26–27).

We no longer use armed forces as our ultimate means of coming out on top; rather, we negotiate by proclaiming peace; by using flatteries; by joining into a league with others and by being deceitful.

Egypt Won with Words

On November 19, 1977 Egyptian President Anwar Sadat visited Jerusalem with peaceable intentions. In

Washington, lies were talked on one table, which resulted in Israel's handing over to Egypt the entire Sinai Peninsula for nothing. Saddat accomplished more with words than his predecessor, Mr. Gamal Abdel Nasser, did with weapons.

Greece or Rome?

Significant about this chapter is that it does not clearly identify the power structure; we don't know whether it refers to the Greek or the Roman rule. Regardless of the exact details, we do know Daniel was referring to our times. What transpired between the kings of the North and South is not as significant in view of what is revealed in verse 28: "Then shall he return into his land with great riches; and his heart shall be against the holy covenant; and he shall do exploits, and return to his own land." The king of the North personifies the Antichrist, revealing his true intention: "his heart shall be against the holy covenant." The covenant is God's eternal written Word and His full counsel to man. The basic principles of that covenant apply to all nations but are being broken worldwide today.

The covenant is God's eternal written Word and His full counsel to man.

Indeed, we are living in the time described in Daniel 2:40: "And the fourth kingdom shall be strong as iron: forasmuch as iron breaketh in pieces and subdueth all things: and as iron that breaketh all these, shall it break in pieces and bruise."

Against the Holy Covenant

This king of the North and his apparent archenemy, the king of the South, remain nameless. History books would indicate that this king was Antiochus Epiphanes. This may well be the case, but it would only be a pre-fulfillment of the prophesied event. "For the ships of Chittim shall come against him: therefore he shall be grieved, and return, and have indignation against the holy covenant: so shall he do; he shall even return, and have intelligence with them that forsake the holy covenant" (verse 30).

The key to understanding this portion of Scripture is the phrase "his heart shall be against the holy covenant." This "holy covenant" is repeated twice: "and have indignation against the holy covenant...and have intelligence with them that forsake the holy covenant."

Forsake the Holy Covenant

The holy covenant began with God and Abraham and was established between God and His people, Israel: "Now the LORD had said unto Abram, Get thee out of thy country, and from thy kindred, and from thy father's house, unto a land that I will shew thee: And I will make of thee a great nation, and I will bless thee, and make thy name great; and thou shalt be a blessing: And I will bless them that bless thee, and curse him that curseth thee: and in thee shall all families of the earth be blessed" (Genesis 12:1–3). This is the covenant of segregation. God told

Abraham to separate from his family, his country, his culture and tradition, and head towards an unknown country. This covenant of separation is according to God's holy will. His intention was to select a family from whom He would bring forth a nation from whom Jesus, the eternal Lamb of God who took away the sins of the world, would be born. This is the holy covenant that God made with man, not vice-versa.

"Be Ye Separate"

This reminds us of our conversion: Nothing mattered more than our heavenly calling when we were saved. Where are we going? This is a spiritual question. Our position before we were called is described in Ephesians 2:12: "That at that time ye were without Christ, being aliens from the commonwealth of Israel, and strangers from the covenants of promise, having no hope, and without God in the world." Note the words "no hope." Now, however, although we don't know our final destination, we do know that Jesus promised: "In my Father's house are many mansions: if it were not so, I would have told you. I go to prepare a place for you. And if I go and prepare a place for you, I will come again, and receive you unto myself; that where I am, there ye may be also" (John 14:2–3). He didn't identify the "Father's house," "the mansions" or "the place." To the Corinthians, Paul wrote: "Eye hath not seen, nor ear heard, neither have entered into the heart of man, the things which God hath prepared for them that love him" (1 Corinthians 2:9). Although we have not yet seen anything, we have faith for the future. What is faith? Hebrews describes it as being "the substance of things hoped for, the evidence of things not seen" (Hebrews 11:1). That is the faith of Abraham, who is called the "father of all believers." He didn't need to witness supernatural phenomena; he simply believed because God had spoken.

Man Wants To Reach God

All religions strive to reach God through their practices and behaviors by implementing countless laws, ordinances, holy days and even sacrifices. Before we read of Abraham's calling, we learn about man's attempt to reach God: "Go to, let us build us a city and a tower, whose top may reach unto heaven; and let us make us a name, lest we be scattered abroad upon the face of the whole earth" (Genesis 11:4). Since then, man has tried to reach God. But God has done the opposite; He came from heaven to earth when He sent His Son in the likeness of man to be given as the supreme, once-and-for-all sacrifice.

Abraham did not make a covenant with God, but God made a covenant with Abraham. The action on Abraham's part was to obey God's instruction to leave his home. That's the only holy covenant that leads to the One who suffered outside the gates of Jerusalem when He carried away the sins of the world.

202

Scripture instructs believers to be separate from this world, to look heavenward to the place where we are "raised...up together and...sit together in heavenly places in Christ Jesus" (Ephesians 2:6). Philippians 3:20 describes the goal of our lives: "For our conversation is in heaven; from whence also we look for the Saviour, the Lord Jesus Christ." This can only become a reality when we have died with Christ, been buried with Him, and ascended with Him into heaven. In that ascended position, "we look for the Saviour, the Lord Jesus Christ."

That's where the holy covenant of segregation made by God with Abraham leads. That is the covenant the world hates. Therefore, the leader described here as the king of the North so vehemently opposes the holy covenant.

Segregation of the Jews

How does the Antichrist succeed? By deception! "He shall even return and have intelligence with them that forsake the holy covenant." The German Menge translation says "his eyes shall be directed favorably towards those who became apostate to the holy covenant."

This has a two-fold interpretation: 1) The Jews always have been segregated whether they liked it or not; however, in these endtimes they are trying to go into the opposite direction. They want to be just another nation, equal to all others. In fact, Israel's Declaration of Independence, dated May 14, 1948 says: "it is moreover the self-evident right of the Jewish people to be a nation as all other nations in its own sovereign state." Further, it states: "We appeal to the United Nations to assist the Jewish people in the building of its State and to admit Israel into the family of nations." This is "apostasy from the holy covenant." It reminds us of Jesus' words recorded in John 5:43: "I am come in my Father's name, and ye receive me not: if another shall come in his own name, him ye will receive." 2) This prophecy is also a revelation about the Church of Jesus Christ. In horror we watch Satan masterfully camouflage his intention through politics and religion so that many within the Church are beginning to forsake the "holy covenant" in favor of political activities. That should not be surprising, for it is prophesied to happen and it is happening even today. This type of deception is carried out in the most reasonable and benevolent manner possible.

The New-Age Model

Is there a system or a model by which the world can be united politically, economically, financially and religiously? The answer is yes! Politically, the ancient Greek/Roman democracy is taking over the world. Economically, free market guided by social/capitalism does not give a chance to any other model. And religiously, Churchianity is forsaking the "holy covenant" of segregation by falling head over heels for anything that looks good, feels good and sounds good.

The Remnant Believers

Another group of believers is mentioned in Daniel 32–34: "but the people that do know their God shall be strong, and do exploits. And they that understand among the people shall instruct many: yet they shall fall by the sword, and by flame, by captivity, and by spoil, many days. Now when they shall fall, they shall be holpen with a little help: but many shall cleave to them with flatteries." History books are filled with accounts of terrible massacres against Christians and Jews throughout the ages. Yes, they did receive "little help," but Scripture says it was only by "flatteries."

This type of persecution will continue until the very end: "And some of them of understanding shall fall, to try them, and to purge, and to make them white, even to the time of the end: because it is yet for a time appointed" (verse 35).

The endtimes began with the founding of the Church of Jesus Christ.

The endtimes began with the founding of the Church of Jesus Christ. The "time appointed" will be when the Church has been completed. That will be the moment when all born-again believers have been raptured into the presence of the Lord to enter the home that was prepared for us before the foundation of the world.

The Self-Willed King

"And the king shall do according to his will; and he

shall exalt himself, and magnify himself above every god, and shall speak marvellous things against the God of gods, and shall prosper till the indignation be accomplished: for that that is determined shall be done" (Daniel 11:36).

This is the last person in the line of these unnamed rulers, the one we believe is the Antichrist. The statement, "in his estate shall stand up," is written for the last time in Daniel 11:21. This is the person described as "a vile person" who will come to power through peace, flatteries and deceit. This "vile person" will turn "against the holy covenant."

Scripture describes him as one who will exalt himself. That statement identifies him as closely related to the father of lies, the originator of sin: "How art thou fallen from heaven, O Lucifer, son of the morning! How art thou cut down to the ground, which didst weaken the nations! For thou hast said in thine heart, I will ascend into heaven, I will exalt my throne above the stars of God: I will sit also upon the mount of the congregation, in the sides of the north: I will ascend above the heights of the clouds; I will be like the most High" (Isaiah 14:12–14).

Self-Deception

This Scripture reveals diabolic self-confidence and therewith it identifies the times in which we live. Just listen to the politicians and their exalted speeches based purely on imagination and self-elevation. The epitome of self-exaltation is also evident in the business world. Take note of the advertisements in the media. One always wants to be greater than the other; each propagates its products with a mixture of truth and lies.

For example, one famous retailer advertises that it "rolls back" prices. Of course, the individual cases are actually true. However, no retailer would be able to exist if all prices were "rolled back" all the time. Needless to say, if a retailer advertised how often it raised prices, people wouldn't patronize its store. Our society is programmed to believe lies that are wrapped up in paper-thin "truth."

Think about the juicy hamburger advertised on television. It's only a picture, but even the picture isn't real because it is not a real hamburger. You can prove that for yourself: Next time you buy a hamburger, take it to a photographer and ask him to

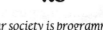

Our society is programmed to believe lies that are wrapped up in paper-thin "truth."

take a picture just like the ones you've seen on television and he will tell you right off the bat that he can't do it because you're showing him the real thing. A photographer can only produce the next best thing – a copy.

Self-Esteem Deception

Churchianity is the biggest culprit. Instead of preaching the Gospel of Jesus Christ, many pastors preach the gospel of self-esteem, peppering their ser-

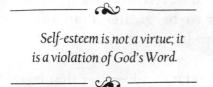

Self-esteem is not a virtue; it is a violation of God's Word.

mons with "pep talks" completely foreign to Scripture. I've heard reports of seminary teachers throughout the world who pump their students with this diabolic teaching of self-esteem. Let me make this clear: Self-esteem is not a virtue; it is a violation of God's Word.

Who Are These Kings?

Are the "kings" in chapter 11 demonic forces or real kings of real countries? According to chapter 10, it seems reasonable to assume they are demonic powers, Satan's guardian angels who stand behind each government.

Such was the case with Persia: "the prince of the kingdom of Persia withstood me one and twenty days" (Daniel 10:13). The messenger who came for the sake of Daniel's prayer mentioned a name, Michael, number one of the chief princes who is a heavenly being and not an earthly creature. Therefore, the powers that withstood the messenger helped by Michael are the powers of darkness in the invisible world.

Here we must consider Ephesians 6:12: "For we wrestle not against flesh and blood, but against principalities, against powers, against the rulers of the darkness of this world, against spiritual wickedness in high places." These principalities, powers and rulers are not leaders or governments of the nations we may identify today, but "evil spirits under the heaven," as translated by Martin Luther.

I cannot reach any other conclusion based on this verse other than the king of the South and the king of the North do not represent earthly kings but are demonic powers, which is why they remain nameless.

Who Is This "Vile" Person?

In proper succession, Daniel was told that after Persia, "The prince of Grecia shall come" (Daniel 10:20). This indicates that every nation has at its head a demonic prince subject to the leadership of Lucifer, also known as "the great dragon...that old serpent, called the Devil, and Satan" (Revelation 12:9).

This "vile person" will speak "marvelous things against the God of gods." This description applies to our times because society today attaches the word "God" to virtually anyone — from politicians to celebrities and occult leaders.

More details are revealed in Daniel 11:37–38: "Neither shall he regard the God of his fathers, nor the desire of women, nor regard any god: for he shall magnify himself above all. But in his estate shall he honour the God of forces: and a god whom his fathers knew not shall he honour with gold, and silver, and with precious stones, and pleasant things."

The God of Forces

Instead of honoring the God of Israel, this person honors the god of forces. This isn't prescribed exclusively for the future, but it also applies to today. It is generally assumed that the Antichrist will establish his kingdom by force; however, this verse says a lot more. All countries of all times have had their borders established by the god of forces.

What is the goal of the god of forces? To receive honor "with gold and silver and precious stones and pleasant things." It is all done for the benefit of one's self.

Verse 39 also refers to our time: "Thus shall he do in the most strong holds with a strange god, whom he shall acknowledge and increase with glory: and he shall cause them to rule over many, and shall divide the land for gain." The god of forces and the god of money are in control of this world, its leaders and the overwhelming majority of the population.

Is He Jewish?

"The God of his fathers" is a typical phraseology in Judaism and a prophetic indication that this person is Jewish. Remember, Jesus said: "I am come in my Father's name, and ye receive me not: if another shall come in his own name, him ye will receive" (John 5:43). He was speaking to His own people, the Jews, in Jerusalem.

Scripture relates that this terrible leader will not desire women, which in itself is a mockery of God's institution of marriage. But in the center of it all, "he shall magnify himself." We don't have to search too far in today's world to see the tendency of self-magnification. This behavior becomes frighteningly apparent in Churchianity, which has been popularized by music that seeks to elevate man to God's level.

The Divided Land

What land is being referred to in verse 39 as being divided for gain? We must keep in mind that Daniel's visions were revealed to him for the sake of his people and his land, not for the Gentile nations. Therefore, we must conclude that the land is Israel, which is further explained in Joel 3:2: "I will also gather all nations, and will bring them down into the valley of Jehoshaphat, and will plead with them there for my people and for my heritage Israel, whom they have scattered among the nations, and parted my land." An accusing finger is being pointed at all nations because they are responsible for parting God's land.

This is a reality today, when all nations are guilty of parting the land of Israel. Not one nation from among more than 200 sovereign countries agrees with the scripturally defined borders of Israel, which extend from the Euphrates River to the river of Egypt. That is Israel's irrevocable inheritance.

These prophecies should not be considered future events because they are in full development today: "He shall enter also into the glorious land, and many countries shall be overthrown: but these shall escape out of his hand, even Edom, and Moab, and the chief of the children of Ammon. He shall stretch forth his hand also upon the countries: and the land of Egypt shall not escape. But he shall have power over the treasures of gold and of silver, and over all the precious things of Egypt: and the Libyans and the Ethiopians shall be at his steps. But tidings out of the east and out of the north shall trouble him: therefore he shall go forth with great fury to destroy, and utterly to make away many" (verses 41–44). Edom, Moab, Ammon, Egypt, Libya and Ethiopia — Arab countries located in the Middle East — are all mentioned. It is in this glorious land of Israel that the Antichrist will make his final appearance.

More Identification of Antichrist

The Apostle Paul identified the Antichrist in 2 Thessalonians 2:4: "Who opposeth and exalteth himself above all that is called God, or that is worshipped; so that he as God sitteth in the temple of God, shewing himself that he is God." He will detest everything that has to do with God

He will detest everything that has to do with God because he will claim to be God and the world will believe him.

because he will claim to be God and the world will believe him.

Center of Abomination

"And he shall plant the tabernacles of his palace between the seas in the glorious holy mountain; yet he shall come to his end, and none shall help him" (Daniel 11:45). The holy mountain mentioned in this verse is Jerusalem, where Solomon's temple once stood. That is the abomination of desolation; the Antichrist will take his place in the temple and attempt to make it his own. Therefore, Revelation calls Jerusalem "Sodom and Egypt, where also our Lord was crucified" (Revelation 11:8).

Light Destroys Darkness

Fortunately, this ruler's occupancy will not last and he will come to an end. How will that occur? "And then shall that Wicked be revealed, whom the Lord shall consume with the spirit of his mouth, and shall destroy with the brightness of his coming" (2 Thessalonians 2:8). Destruction does not come by power or might but by "the spirit of his mouth." Light will always destroy darkness!

Chapter 13

THE END OF THE VISION

"And at that time shall Michael stand up, the great prince which standeth for the children of thy people: and there shall be a time of trouble, such as never was since there was a nation even to that same time: and at that time thy people shall be delivered, every one that shall be found written in the book" (Daniel 12:1).

When will Michael, the great prince, stand up for the children of Israel? At the time the previous verse is fulfilled: "And he shall plant the tabernacles of his palace between the

seas in the glorious holy mountain; yet he shall come to his end, and none shall help him" (Daniel 11:45). Those are the end stages of the endtimes.

Antichrist To Come

The Antichrist will reach his end when he is confronted by the Prince of Light, confirmed by 2 Thessalonians 2:8: "And then shall that Wicked be revealed, whom the Lord shall consume with the spirit of his mouth, and shall destroy with the brightness of his coming." The big lie will be exposed the instant Jesus appears and this revelation in itself is the center of the Antichrist's destruction.

Before Antichrist Comes

The Antichrist cannot come unless preparation has been made for him. First John 2:18 says: "Little children, it is the last time: and as ye have heard that antichrist shall come, even now are there many antichrists; whereby we know that it is the last time." This was written almost 2,000 years ago; preparation for his arrival has been going on for that long.

The Antichrist is a spoke in the wheel of the devil's

strategy, so we must be careful to not place him only in the framework of the seven-year Tribulation; however, he will be manifested during that particular time. When the light and the salt of the earth have been removed, spiritual darkness will prevail and the time will come for him to take the stage. But it stands to reason that he cannot appear unless certain developments have taken place.

Each nation has a role to play and each one is ruled by Satan's demons. From that perspective we understand why, for example, there was a Dark Ages in Europe and why there were two world wars. These events helped establish world unity in preparation of the coming Antichrist.

> *When the light and the salt of the earth have been removed, spiritual darkness will prevail and the time will come for him to take the stage.*

Daniel prophesied that the Antichrist's dominion would be global, which corresponds with the teaching of the New Testament. A global government cannot exist unless preparations are made for it. So we see that both world wars contributed to the unification of the nations — moreso than any other events in history. For example, without technological inventions it would be impossible for the Antichrist to rule the world or to effectively communicate.

When we understand that demon princes and kings from the invisible world rule the nations, we can start to understand that born-again believers have no future here. There would be no escape if we remained on earth; we must be removed by God's supernatural intervention.

Preparation by Deception

How do we know the Antichrist is preparing for his appearance? "They went out from us, but they were not of us; for if they had been of us, they would no doubt have continued with us: but they went out, that they might be made manifest that they were not all of us" (1 John 2:19). We are wasting our time if we think the Antichrist will come from among the Muslims, Hindus, Buddhists or the atheists. He will come from within Churchianity.

How is it possible for the epitome of evil to come from apostate Churchianity? Because the overwhelming majority of Churchianity doesn't really believe the Word of God.

But the Word of God explains its power: "For the word of God is quick, and powerful, and sharper than any two-edged sword, piercing even to the dividing asunder of soul and spirit, and of the joints and marrow, and is a discerner of the thoughts and intents of the heart" (Hebrews 4:12). This is very important. The Word of God is able to separate the soul from the spirit. Man consists of a spirit, a soul and a body. The spirit that becomes born again is vertically directed, as documented in Philippians 3:20: "For our conversation is in heaven; from whence also we look for the Saviour, the Lord Jesus Christ." The soul, on the other hand, is horizontally directed; that is, it relates to the things of this world. This reveals the great tragedy of our day; there are too many "soulish" Christians who are easily swayed by each new movement and every new sensation. One newspaper reporter mockingly wrote this about the premiere of *The Passion of the Christ*: "The promised revival prophesied by prominent church leaders fell flat on its face." Why? Because it was not the sharp, two-edged sword of the Word of God. It was a cheap imitation of the truth; sinful man played a game and produced a fictitious portrayal of the crucifixion. The irony is that people will watch an incorrect account rather than read the accurate and truthful biblical account as recorded in the Gospels. Churchianity has an easier time believing Mel Gibson than the Holy Spirit-inspired, two-edged sword that is God's Word!

Two Views

All developments in our time are leading toward the Antichrist, the endtimes, Armageddon and the Great Tribulation. But when we analyze the state of the world

Churchianity has an easier time believing Mel Gibson than the Holy Spirit-inspired, two-edged sword that is God's Word!

from an earthly perspective, we have to agree things are better than ever.

Jesus compared our time with Noah's: "As it was in the days of Noe, so shall it be also in the days of the Son of man. They did eat, they drank, they married wives, they were given in marriage, until the day that Noe entered into the ark, and the flood came, and destroyed them all" (Luke 17:26–27). Jesus listed normal daily activities. Of course, eating, drinking and getting married aren't sins; however, one sin was mentioned: "they...knew not." In other words they were unaware of God's plans. They ignored the prophetic Word and all perished as a result.

Our time is marked by this "knew not" attitude expressed by an unprecedented compulsion for material gain. The god of this world offers the greatest luxuries people have ever seen; however, the world is ignorant of the preparations taking place for the sudden removal of the Church before the "flood," i.e. the Great Tribulation, comes upon the world!

Destructive Judgment

What will this terrible "time of trouble" be? The extent of these troubles are revealed in the book of Revelation, expressed in the seven seals, the seven trumpets and the seven vials. This catastrophic event will be global. Revelation 6:8 says: "And power was given unto them over the fourth part of the earth, to kill with sword, and with hunger, and with death, and with the beasts of the earth." Note the words "of the earth." This is reinforced in verse 15, where we read: "And the kings of the earth." Clearly, this will be a time of unprecedented global trouble.

When the seventh seal is opened, we will see judgment upon a third of the world. One-third of the vegetation will burn up (Revelation 8:7), one-third of the seas will turn to blood, one-third of all marine life and one-third of all ships will be destroyed (verse 9), and one-third part of all rivers and fountains will be poisoned (verse 12). As a result, "many men died of the waters, because they were made bitter" (verse 11). Revelation 9:15 says: "for to slay the third part of men." According to today's statistics, that would be more than 2 billion people, or seven times the population of the United States. Again in verse 18 we read: "By these three was the third part of men killed, by the fire, and by the smoke, and by the brimstone."

This is just a small glimpse of the judgments that will befall planet Earth. I don't think we need to look for earthly manifestations such as nuclear weapons or biological wars, because this judgment will be made by God. This is confirmed in Revelation 16:9: "And men were scorched with great heat, and blasphemed the name of God, which hath power over these plagues: and they repented not to give him glory." The people alive at this time will have recognized that the catastrophe that has befallen them originated with God, whom they will blaspheme as a result.

What Will Happen to Israel?

What will happen to Israel? We learned in chapter 9 that the center for the prophetic vision Daniel received primarily concerned the people of Israel: "I am come to make thee understand what shall befall thy people in the latter days" (Daniel 10:14). While the world is receiving judgment and being destroyed, Israel will be judged with a judgment that leads to salvation.

> *While the world is receiving judgment and being destroyed, Israel will be judged with a judgment that leads to salvation.*

Israel will be deceived and follow in the footsteps of the Antichrist, but not to the end. Here we see an amazing act of God's grace: Michael, the archangel, will interfere for the sake of the Jews.

Jacob's Trouble

God will interfere on behalf of His people during the Great Tribulation by sending Michael the archangel. Here is what will happen: "And at that time thy people shall be delivered, every one that shall be found written in the book" (Daniel 12:1). This corresponds with the prophecies recorded in the book of Jeremiah, who also spoke of the day when God will pour out His wrath upon the earth: "Alas! For that day is great, so that none is like it: it is even the time of Jacob's trouble; but he shall be saved out of it" (Jeremiah 30:7).

The Final Judgment

Daniel 12:2 goes far beyond the Great Tribulation and the 1,000-year kingdom of peace: "And many of them that sleep in the dust of the earth shall awake, some to everlasting life, and some to shame and everlasting contempt" (Daniel 12:2). That refers to the final resurrection. Those who will be resurrected to everlasting life belong to the first resurrection, which encompasses all the resurrections, including the Rapture. The others who are resurrected will stand before the Great White Throne and will be judged unto condemnation.

The Coming Reward

Then we read, "And they that be wise shall shine as the brightness of the firmament; and they that turn many to righteousness as the stars for ever and ever" (Daniel 12:3). This verse contains such a tremendous promise for those who occupy themselves with the righteousness of God, revealed in the endtimes through Jesus Christ. Whatever you do and have done for the sake of the Lord will not lose its reward. The "wise shall shine as the brightness of the firmament."

> *Whatever you do and have done for the sake of the Lord will not lose its reward.*

The Sealed Book

"But thou, O Daniel, shut up the words, and seal the book, even to the time of the end: many shall run to and fro, and knowledge shall be increased" (Daniel 12:4). This is such a misunderstood verse. What does it mean to "seal the book"? The book is to be shut up until the time of the end. This does not refer to the end of the world, but to the end of time. How do we know we are in the endtimes? Because the verse speaks of the deliverance of the Jews.

John the Baptist's father, Zecharias, revealed this in his prophecy "To give knowledge of salvation unto his people by the remission of their sins" (Luke 1:77). The sealed book was opened with the revelation of that knowledge. Yet Israel did not see, hear or understand. Read what the prophet Isaiah wrote in 760 B.C.: "Go, and tell this people, Hear ye indeed, but understand not; and see ye indeed, but perceive not. Make the heart of this people fat, and make their ears heavy, and shut their eyes; lest they see with their eyes, and hear with their ears, and understand with their heart, and convert, and be healed" (Isaiah 6:9–10). The King was in their midst, ready to establish the kingdom of God on earth, but they didn't want to believe.

The Sealed Book for the Gentiles

There was a reason for this: the Gentiles. God already had promised Abraham, "in thee shall all families of the earth be blessed" (Genesis 12:3). The fulfillment is recorded in Romans 4:16: "Therefore it is of faith, that it might be by grace; to the end the promise might be sure to all the seed; not to that only which is of the law, but to that also which is

The Gospel message has been preached around the world for 2,000 years but the majority of people have rejected it.

224

of the faith of Abraham; who is the father of us all."

The Gospel message has been preached around the world for 2,000 years but the majority of people have rejected it. In fact, the world has persecuted the Jewish people, from whom this salvation originates. Jesus said, "Salvation is of the Jews." Approximately 14 million Jews have been killed since the destruction of the temple in 70 A.D. The most horrific slaughter was initiated by Adolf Hitler's Nazi Germany, which slaughtered more than 6 million Jews.

What about today? No nation agrees with God's promise to Abraham that the Holy Land, from the Euphrates River to the river of Egypt, belongs to the Jews. This mentality confirms that all nations oppose the God of creation, the God of Israel, and that they collectively reject the message of salvation.

Science and Travel on the Rise

Next comes an important statement: "Many shall run to and fro, and knowledge shall be increased" (Daniel 12:4). While this has been interpreted in various ways, one thing is clear: It is a prophecy anyone could have made in the past as well as in the present. Mankind will continue in his progress, traveling to and fro and learn more and more. However, this verse also contains a great prophetic message that Jesus used to warn about the endtimes: "For as in the days that were before the flood they were eating and drinking, marrying and giving in marriage, until the day that Noe entered into the ark, And knew not until the flood came, and took them all away; so shall also the coming of the Son of man be" (Matthew 24:38–39). Normal daily activity without making preparation is the key to understanding the danger of the endtimes.

The world has made tremendous progress in science and technology and we do indeed travel more than ever. But we are neglecting something: the prophetic Word: "Therefore be ye also ready: for in such an hour as ye think not the Son of man cometh" (Matthew 24:44).

Chapter 14

MYSTERY FOR THE ENDTIMES

"But go thou thy way till the end be: for thou shalt rest, and stand in thy lot at the end of the days" (Daniel 12:13).

The book of four visions Daniel wrote was now closed. In verse 4 he was instructed to "shut up the words, and seal the book, even to the time of the end."

What Was This Book About?

First of all, the book outlined the fulfillment of Jeremiah's prophecies, among others who spoke of Israel's coming defeat, the destruction of Jerusalem and the temple, and the subsequent captivity in Babylon.

Second, the book of Daniel revealed the future of the Gentile world. Realizing this indeed makes it easier to understand Daniel's prophecies. We must not add any kingdoms or power structures to these four. That is the beginning and the end of the Gentile nations. These four represent the entire world and according to Daniel 2:44, they will be replaced by God's kingdom: "And in the days of these kings shall the God of heaven set up a kingdom, which shall never be destroyed: and the kingdom shall not be left to other people, but it shall break in pieces and consume all these kingdoms, and it shall stand for ever."

Third, and chiefly, the book described the future of Daniel's people. Michael the archangel said: "I am come to make thee understand what shall befall thy people in the latter days" (Daniel 10:14). The people of Israel received a special promise — the coming of Michael their defender, "and at that time thy people shall be delivered" (Daniel 12:1).

228

Two Messengers

However, after the book was sealed, we read: "Then I Daniel looked, and, behold, there stood other two, the one on this side of the bank of the river, and the other on that side of the bank of the river. And one said to the man clothed in linen, which was upon the waters of the river, How long shall it be to the end of these wonders?" (verses 5–6). These two heavenly beings positioned on opposite sides of the river remain unidentified.

One has a question: "How long shall it be to the end of these wonders?" The Tanakh translates this as: "How long until the end of these awful things?" This heavenly being was asking about the duration of the Great Tribulation. He received the answer in the next verse: "And I heard the man clothed in linen, which was upon the waters of the river, when he held up his right hand and his left hand unto heaven, and sware by him that liveth for ever that it shall be for a time, times, and an half; and when he shall have accomplished to scatter the power of the holy people, all these things shall be finished." (verse 7). This corresponds to the last part of Daniel 7:25: "And they shall be given into his hand until a time and times and the dividing of time," which corresponds to the latter half of the seven-year Tribulation.

Jerusalem and the Gentiles

Did this heavenly messenger not know the answer, or did he ask so that Daniel would receive the answer? The question seemed to be directed to Daniel, for he confessed: "I heard, but I understood not" (verse 8).

An interesting phrase follows: "to scatter the power of the holy people." We know "the holy people" are the Jews (regardless of their condition, their position from God's perspective is defined in Deuteronomy 14:2). Thus our question should be: When was this fulfilled? Or is it yet to be fulfilled?

Let's read what Jesus said about the Great Tribulation in Luke 21:24: "And they shall fall by the edge of the sword, and shall be led away captive into all nations: and Jerusalem shall be trodden down of the Gentiles, until the times of the Gentiles be fulfilled." Note that this prophecy began to be fulfilled in 70 A.D. when Jerusalem was destroyed and the Jews were literally led captive into all nations.

With reasonable assurance we can say that the captivity ended May 14, 1948, when Israel was established as a nation and many Jews took the opportunity to return to the land of their fathers.

But there is more to it, because Jesus said Jerusalem would be under the authority of the Gentiles until the times of the Gentiles are fulfilled. The Gentiles most certainly are treading down Jerusalem today. The Jews don't even have the right to determine their capital city. For example, the United States has an embassy in Tel Aviv, not in Jerusalem. Virtually all nations with which Israel has diplomatic relations place their embassies in Tel Aviv because they do not recognize Jerusalem as the capital city of Israel. For all practical purposes, Jerusalem is a divided city because of the Gentiles. They determine the state of that city and will continue to be the final authority: "until the times of the Gentiles be fulfilled."

Amazingly, Daniel did not understand. He testified: "And I heard, but I understood not: then said I, O my Lord, what shall be the end of these things?" (verse 8). Thus, the interpretation of his own book was closed to himself. Again, he was instructed: "Go thy way, Daniel: for the words are closed up and sealed till the time of the end" (verse 9).

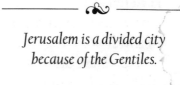

Jerusalem is a divided city because of the Gentiles.

When Will the Book Be Opened?

I venture to say the opening or the beginning of the fulfillment of the hidden parts of division was revealed when Jesus came. He is the fulfillment, the ultimate revelation. Nothing is hidden before Him; that which is secret is open, He is the beginning and the end. Thus, with the proclamation of the Gospel of Jesus Christ, confirmed by the baptism of the Holy Spirit, the time of the revelation of Daniel's sealed book of visions began. This, however, will continue until the book of the seven seals is opened.

We read about that in Revelation 5:5: "And one of the elders saith unto me, Weep not: behold, the Lion of the tribe of Judah, the Root of David, hath prevailed to open the book, and to loose the seven seals thereof." It is significant, however, that in Revelation 6:1 we read: "And I saw when the Lamb opened one of the seals, and I heard, as it were the noise of thunder, one of the four beasts saying, Come and see." The Lamb, not the Lion of the tribe of Judah, actually opens the book. That image goes against what we might commonly assume. After all, the lion is king of the jungle while the lamb is a picture of innocence; it is defenseless. The fact that the Lamb opens up the seal gives us a glimpse of the other side of the Lamb of God, who was slain before the foundation of the world. That other side is His wrath: "And the kings of the earth, and the great men, and the rich men, and the chief captains, and the mighty men, and every bondman, and every free man, hid themselves in the dens and in the rocks of the mountains; And said to the mountains and rocks, Fall on us, and hide us from the face of him that sitteth on the throne, and from the wrath of the Lamb" (Revelation 6:15–16).

People will then recognize that the Lamb who paid for their sin on Calvary's cross has become the One who cast the unforgiven sin of man onto their heads, thus "the wrath of the Lamb."

The Endtimes

Then we read a prophecy about a particular time: "Many shall be purified, and made white, and tried; but the wicked shall do wickedly: and none of the wicked shall understand; but the wise shall understand" (verse 10). Here we see a parallel to the words of John the Revelator: "He that is unjust, let him be unjust still: and he which is filthy, let him be filthy still: and he that is righteous, let him be righteous still: and he that is holy, let him be holy still" (Revelation 22:11).

The Time Table

Next, we receive a prophetic time table: "from the time that the daily sacrifice shall be taken away, and the abomination that maketh desolate set up, there shall be a thousand two hundred and ninety days. Blessed is he that waiteth, and cometh to the thousand three hundred and five and thirty days" (Daniel 12:11–12). The last half of the Tribulation —3 ½ years — equals 1,260 days. What is the significance of the additional 45 days? This is the time of the implementation of

The nations must be judged before the Millennium can begin for them.

the 1,000-year kingdom of peace. We have to keep in mind that the nations must be judged before the Millennium can begin for them.

Judgment of Egypt

Let us consider the land of Egypt: The prophet Ezekiel wrote: "And the land of Egypt shall be desolate and waste; and they shall know that I am the LORD: because he hath said, The river is mine, and

I have made it. Behold, therefore I am against thee, and against thy rivers, and I will make the land of Egypt utterly waste and desolate, from the tower of Syene even unto the border of Ethiopia. No foot of man shall pass through it, nor foot of beast shall pass through it, neither shall it be inhabited forty years. And I will make the land of Egypt desolate in the midst of the countries that are desolate, and her cities among the cities that are laid waste shall be desolate forty years: and I will scatter the Egyptians among the nations, and will disperse them through the countries" (Ezekiel 29:9–12). No scriptural or historical evidence indicates that this portion of prophecy has been fulfilled; therefore, it is still future.

The seven-year Tribulation period will commence immediately following the Rapture of the Church. After the Tribulation, Jesus will establish His 1,000-year kingdom of peace for Israel, but the nations will still have to be judged.

It seems as though Egypt will have to wait 40 years before verses 13–14 are fulfilled: "Yet thus saith the Lord GOD; At the end of forty years will I gather the Egyptians from the people whither they were scattered. And I will bring again the captivity of Egypt, and will cause them to return into the land of Pathros, into the land of their habitation; and they shall be there a base kingdom."

Blessing of the Arabs

There is a blessing yet to be fulfilled for the Arabs

as well. This was prophesied by Isaiah, who wrote: "In that day shall there be a highway out of Egypt to Assyria, and the Assyrian shall come into Egypt, and the Egyptian into Assyria, and the Egyptians shall serve with the Assyrians. In that day shall Israel be the third with Egypt and with Assyria, even a blessing in the midst of the land: Whom the LORD of hosts shall bless, saying, Blessed be Egypt my people, and Assyria the work of my hands, and Israel mine inheritance" (Isaiah 19:23–25).

God, the Creator of heaven and earth, will restore but He will do it in His own way and in His own time, and not before destructive judgment comes upon the nations and judgment that leads to salvation comes to Israel.

The Final Revelation

Daniel received no more revelation but was encouraged with these words: "But go thou thy way till the end be: for thou shalt rest, and stand in thy lot at the end of the days." In other words, "Well done, thou good and faithful servant, your reward is yet to come!"

May this desire be reborn in each of our hearts as we strive toward the things of the Lord so that He pronounces those words to you and I when we enter eternity.